Fodor's 1st

Pocket
Buenos Aires

Excerpted from *Fodor's Argentina*

Fodor's Travel Publications
New York • Toronto • London • Sydney • Auckland
www.fodors.com

Fodor's Pocket Buenos Aires

EDITOR: Amy Karafin
Editorial Contributors: Laura Kidder, Natasha Lesser, Kristen Masick
Editorial Production: Rebecca Zeiler
Maps: David Lindroth, *cartographer*; Rebecca Baer and Bob Blake, *map editors*
Design: Fabrizio La Rocca, *creative director*; Guido Caroti, *art director*; Jolie Novak, *photo editor*
Cover Photo: Fernando Bueno/The Image Bank
Cover Design: Lyndell Brookhouse-Gil
Production/Manufacturing: Mike Costa

Copyright

First Edition
ISBN 0–679–00487–4
ISSN 1527–4934

Special Sales

Fodor's Travel Publications are available at special discounts for bulk purchases for sales promotions or premiums. Special editions, including personalized covers, excerpts of existing guides, and corporate imprints, can be created in large quantities for special needs. For more information, contact your local bookseller or write to Special Markets, Fodor's Travel Publications, 201 East 50th Street, New York, NY 10022. Inquiries from Canada should be directed to your local Canadian bookseller or sent to Random House of Canada, Ltd., Marketing Department, 2775 Matheson Boulevard East, Mississauga, Ontario L4W 4P7. Inquiries from the United Kingdom should be sent to Fodor's Travel Publications, 20 Vauxhall Bridge Road, London SW1V 2SA, England.

PRINTED IN THE UNITED STATES OF AMERICA

10 9 8 7 6 5 4 3 2 1

Important Tip

Although all prices, opening times, and other details in this book are based on information supplied to us at press time, changes occur all the time in the travel world, and Fodor's cannot accept responsibility for facts that become outdated or for inadvertent errors or omissions. So **always confirm information when it matters,** especially if you're making a detour to visit a specific place.

CONTENTS

Maps

ON THE ROAD WITH FODOR'S

THE TRIPS YOU take this year and next are going to be significant trips, if only because they'll be your first in the new millennium. Acutely aware of that fact, we've pulled out all stops in preparing *Fodor's Pocket Buenos Aires*. To direct you to the places that are truly worth your time and money in these important years, we've rallied the team of endearingly picky know-it-alls we're pleased to call our writers. Having seen all corners of Buenos Aires, they're real experts. If you knew them, you'd poll them for tips yourself.

After graduating from Boston University with a degree in International Studies, **Kristen Masick** set off for Latin America. She ended up living in Buenos Aires for two years, managing press relations for the Embassy of Nigeria. While there, she also wrote about Buenos Aires for this guide.

Don't Forget to Write

Keeping a travel guide fresh and up-to-date is a big job. So we love your feedback—positive and negative—and follow up on all suggestions. Contact the Pocket Buenos Aires editor at editors@ fodors.com or c/o Fodor's, 201 East 50th Street, New York, New York 10022. And have a wonderful trip!

Karen Cure

Karen Cure

Editorial Director

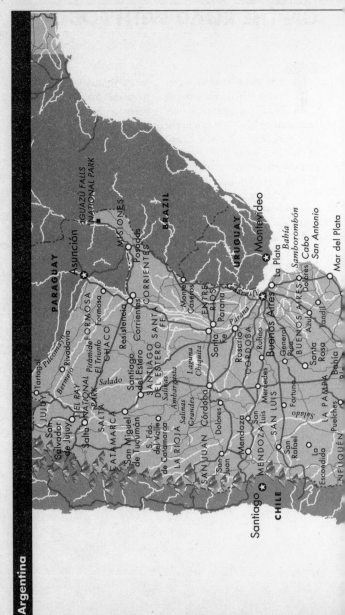

Argentina

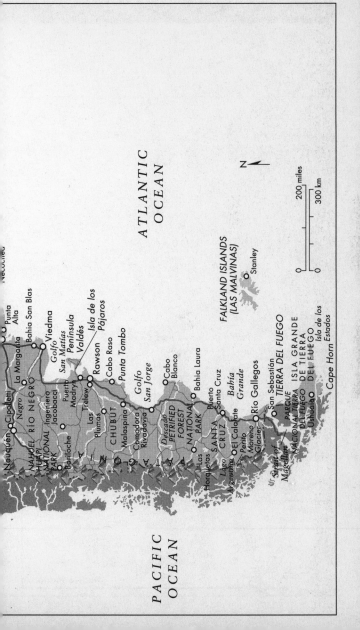

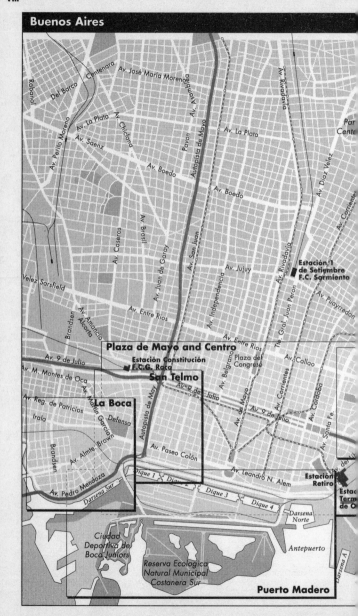

SMART TRAVEL TIPS

AIR TRAVEL

For international flights, **the major gateway to Argentina is Buenos Aires's Ezeiza International Airport,** 34 km (21 mi) and 45 minutes from the city center. Ezeiza International Airport is served by a variety of foreign airlines, as well as domestic airlines that run international routes. Though Argentina has other international airports, they generally only serve flights from other South American countries. If your national airline does not fly directly into Buenos Aires, it's often possible to fly into Brazil, and take a two–three hour flight on Aerolineas Argentinas into Ezeiza. Miami and New York are the primary departure points for flights to Argentina from the United States.

Major sights in Argentina are often very far apart, and long-distance transportation overland can be slow; you'll probably be traveling around the country by plane if you're short on time. Note that it's often necessary to fly back to Buenos Aires in order to get to your next point (even if it's in the same region as the place you departed from).

Keep in mind that **flights from Buenos Aires to other points within Argentina depart from Aeroparque Jorge Newbury** in Belgrano, more than 60 km (38 mi) from the international airport. A taxi ride from the Aeroparque to the center of Buenos Aires should cost less than $10 and, without much traffic, should take about 15–25 minutes. Note that in winter the number of flights to tourist destinations is greatly reduced.

➤ AIRPORTS: **Aeroparque Jorge Newbury** (☎ 11/4773–9805). **Ezeiza Airport** (☎ 11/4480–0217).

CARRIERS

➤ DOMESTIC AND INTERNATIONAL AIRLINES: **Aerolineas Argentinas** (☎ 800/333–0276 in U.S.; 11/4340–3777 or 11/4961–9361 in Buenos Aires). **Aeroperu** (☎ 800/777–7717). **American Airlines** (☎ 800/433–7300 in the U.S.; 11/4480–0366 in Buenos Aires). **Austral** (☎ 11/4317–3605 in Buenos Aires). **LanChile** (☎ 800/735–5526 in the U.S.; 11/4312–8161 in Buenos Aires). **LAPA** (☎ 11/4912–1008 in Buenos Aires). **United Airlines** (☎ 800/538–2929 in the U.S.; 11/4316–0777 in

Buenos Aires). **Varig Brasil** (☎ 800/468–2744 in the U.S.; 11/4342–4420 in Buenos Aires). **Vasp** (☎ 800/732–8277 in the U.S.; 11/4311–1135 in Buenos Aires).

➤ U.K. TO ARGENTINA: **American Airlines** (☎ 0345/789–789) from London Heathrow via Miami or New York. **British Airways** (☎ 0345/222–111) from London Gatwick. **Iberia** (☎ 0171/830–0011 in U.K.; 11/4327–2739 in Buenos Aires) via Madrid. **Virgin Atlantic** (☎ 01293/747–747) from Gatwick to Miami, with connections there.

CHECK-IN & BOARDING

Remember to **bring your passport.** You'll be asked to show it when you check in and at customs in Argentina as well as upon your return home.

CUTTING COSTS

Always **check different routings** and look into using different airports. Travel agents, especially low-fare specialists (☞ Discounts & Deals, *below*), are helpful.

Consolidators are another good source. Carefully read the fine print detailing penalties for changes and cancellations, and **confirm your consolidator reservation with the airline.**

➤ CONSOLIDATORS: **Cheap Tickets** (☎ 800/377–1000). **Discount Airline Ticket Service** (☎ 800/576–1600). **Unitravel** (☎ 800/325–2222). **Up & Away Travel** (☎

212/889–2345). **World Travel Network** (☎ 800/409–6753).

ENJOYING THE FLIGHT

Traveling between the Americas is a bit less tiring than to Europe or Asia because there's less of a time difference and thus less jet lag. New York, for instance, is only one time zone behind Buenos Aires in summer (it's two in winter, as Argentina does not observe American daylight savings time), and there's only a four-hour difference between Los Angeles and Buenos Aires. Flights are generally overnight to Buenos Aires, so you can plan on sleeping while flying.

If you happen to be taking Lan-Chile from the United States, you must change planes in Santiago, which means you'll probably get a lovely view of the Andes on your connecting flight to Buenos Aires. Southbound, the best views are usually out the windows on the left side of the plane.

For more legroom **request an emergency-aisle seat.** Don't sit in the row in front of the emergency aisle or in front of a bulkhead, where seats may not recline. If you have dietary concerns, **ask for special meals when booking.**

Most carriers prohibit smoking throughout their systems; others allow smoking only on certain routes or even certain departures from that route, so **contact your carrier regarding its smoking policy.** Note that smoking is common throughout Latin America, so be sure to ask especially when flying a Latin-American carrier.

FLYING TIMES

Flying times to Buenos Aires are 11–12 hours from New York and 8½ hours from Miami. Flights from Los Angeles are often routed through either Lima, Bogotá, or Miami.

HOW TO COMPLAIN

If your baggage goes astray or your flight goes awry, complain right away. Most carriers require that you **file a claim immediately.**

➤ AIRLINE COMPLAINTS: **U.S. Department of Transportation Aviation Consumer Protection Division** (✉ C-75, Room 4107, Washington, DC 20590, ☎ 202/ 366–2220). **Federal Aviation Administration Consumer Hotline** (☎ 800/322–7873).

RECONFIRMING

Always **reconfirm your flight,** even if you have a ticket and a reservation. On the majority of routes in Argentina, flights are fully booked—usually with passengers with a lot of baggage to check-in. Many Argentinians arrive at the airport minutes before takeoff— you're best off avoiding this custom. Always **arrive at the airport well in advance of takeoff** to allow for the lengthy check-in. When leaving Argentina, you'll need to show your passport and pay a departure tax of about $20,

either in pesos or dollars.

AIRPORT TRANSFERS

TRANSFERS

Bus, taxi, and *remis* (a kind of taxi or car service for which the price of a ride is pre-arranged) service is available from Buenos Aires's Ezeiza International Airport. Remis tickets can be purchased from the well-marked transportation counter in the airport. Regular taxi service from the airport to downtown costs at least $35. City buses ($2) operate on a regular schedule, but the ride takes close to two hours and there's a limit of two bags. A 24-hour private bus service is run by Mañuel Tienda León to all downtown hotels ($15); buses depart from the airport on scheduled intervals throughout the day. For the trip to the airport, Tienda León provides frequent van service from its office in front of the Obelisk and from other locations throughout the city. It's a reliable service and nearly as fast as a taxi, but costs about half the price.

BOAT & FERRY TRAVEL

Hydrofoils and ferries cross the Río de la Plata between Buenos Aires and Uruguay several times a day. Boats often sell out quickly, particularly on summer weekends, so it's important to book tickets at least a few days in advance. This can be done by going to the dock or ticket sales office, or by reserving tickets with a credit card via phone. The most popular company, with the most frequent service, is Buquebus. Buquebus provides service for passengers and their vehicles between Buenos Aires and Colonia, Montevideo, Piriápolis, and Punta del Este in Uruguay. The 2½-hour ride between Buenos Aires and Montevideo costs about $110 (round-trip) for tourist class and $140 for first class. The cheaper and slower (and less environmentally sound) ferry plies between Buenos Aires and Colonia and costs about $55, round-trip. Ferry Lineas Argentina also serves the Buenos Aires–Uruguay route on a smaller scale with fewer boats each day. American cruiseliners occasionally continue on to Argentina from Brazil. Yachting is extremely popular along the coast, though boat rentals are difficult to find.

➤ BOAT & FERRY INFORMATION: **Buquebus** (✉ Av. Córdoba and Av. Madero; ✉ in Patio Bullrich shopping mall, ☎ 11/4317–1001). **Ferry Lineas Argentina** (✉ Florida 780, ☎ 11/4314–5100).

BUS TRAVEL

There are generally two types of long-distance buses: *comun* and *diferencial*. On comun buses, the cheaper option, you'll usually get a seat, but it may not be that comfortable and there may not be air-conditioning or heating. Diferencial, only marginally more expensive, usually have reclining seats (some even have *coche-camas,* bedlike seats), an attendant, and snacks. To get between neighboring towns, you can generally catch a local city bus. On many long-distance trips, videos are shown.

Buenos Aires's Estación Terminal de Omnibus is the main gateway for long-distance and international bus travel. Over 60 bus companies are housed in the station, which may seem overwhelming and confusing at first. But there's a logic to what appears to be chaos: bus-company stands are arranged not in order of company name, but by destinations served. In general, different companies serving the same destination are clumped together, making it easy to compare times and prices. Mañuel Tienda León provides frequent and dependable bus service between Buenos Aires and all Argentina's provinces as well as neighboring countries.

Tickets can be purchased at bus terminals right up until departure time. Note that in larger cities there may be different terminals for buses to different destinations. Arrive early to get a ticket, and **be prepared to pay cash.** On holidays, buy your ticket as far in advance as possible and arrive at the station extra early.

When traveling by bus, **bring your own food and beverages,** though food stops are usually made en route. Travel light, dress comfortably, and **keep a close eye on your belongings.**

Colectivos (local buses) run all over the city. Routes are marked on blue signs at bus stops, and the fare is required in exact change. Fares are based on destination—the minimum fare is 65¢, and the typical ride through the city is about 70¢. There is also a more comfortable and expensive bus called the *diferencial* (stated on a sign on the front of the bus), which is climate controlled and on which you are assured a seat; it costs about $2 for an average city ride and runs less frequently.

As you board the bus, tell the driver your destination, and he'll tell you what fare to drop into the machine next to him. The machine will print a ticket, which you must keep throughout your journey on the bus as (theoretically) it can be collected any time. Drivers are usually nice enough to tell you where to get off. If they happen to forget, you can be sure that the locals on the bus will remind you, since foreigners are often an object of (gentle) curiosity on city buses. City buses run all night, but with far less frequency (sometimes only once an hour) after midnight.

➤ LONG-DISTANCE BUS SERVICE: **Mañuel Tienda León** (✉ Santa Fe 790, Buenos Aires, ☎ 11/4383–4454).

FARES & SCHEDULES
Purchase tickets in the bus terminal before boarding. Ticket prices depend on the bus company and destination. For longer trips, **it's worth comparing bus prices with airfares,** as it's not always that much cheaper to take the bus.

➤ BUS INFORMATION: **Estación Terminal de Omnibus** (✉ Av. Ramos Mejía 1680, Buenos Aires, ☎ 11/4310–0700).

RESERVATIONS
You can make reservations on buses, though it's not really necessary (except on holiday weekends); there are always plenty of bus companies going to the same destinations.

BUSINESS HOURS
Official business hours are 9–7 for offices and 9–4 for banks. That said, don't count on anyone actually being in the office before 10. Note, too, that the lunch hour is long, generally at least and hour and a half.

GAS STATIONS
The majority of gas stations in Buenos Aires, other cities, resort areas, and along the highway close at midnight and open again early in the morning, though it's possible to find some stations open 24 hours. In the suburbs, gas stations are generally open until about 9 PM. In rural areas, gas station hours are much less consistent.

MUSEUMS & SIGHTS
Most museums are open only five days a week, generally from Tuesday to Saturday, though sometimes from Wednesday to Sunday.

POST OFFICES AND TELECENTROS

Post offices are open weekdays 8–6 and Saturday 8–1. Most Tele-centros, offices where you can make long-distance calls or send faxes, are open 7:30 AM–midnight.

SHOPS

Shops are open late (from 10 often until 9) and on Sunday to compete with the malls. Outside Buenos Aires, stores tend to be open from 10 until 6 or 7 and close for the weekend from 1 Saturday through Sunday (including food shops).

CAMERAS & PHOTOGRAPHY

EQUIPMENT PRECAUTIONS

Before departing, you may want to **register your foreign-made camera or laptop with U.S. Customs** (☞ Customs & Duties, *below*). At the very least, if you plan to use your equipment in Argentina, it's a good idea to register it at customs upon entering the country.

Always **be prepared to turn on your camera or camcorder** to prove to security personnel that the device is real. It's a good idea to ask for hand inspection of film, which becomes clouded after successive exposures to airport X-ray machines, and **keep videotapes away from metal detectors.**

Carry an extra supply of batteries. It's also a good idea to **keep your equipment in resealable plastic bags.**

FILM & DEVELOPING

It's very easy to find places to purchase and develop film in Buenos Aires. Prices and quality are about equal to those in the United States.

PHOTO ADVICE

The higher the altitude, the greater the proportion of ultraviolet rays. Light meters do not read these rays and consequently, except for close-ups or full-frame portraits where the reading is taken directly off the subject, photos may be overexposed. If you'll be visiting the Andes, **get a skylight (81B or 81C) or polarizing filter to minimize haze and light problems.** These filters may also help with the glare caused by white adobe buildings and sandy beaches.

➤ PHOTO HELP: **Kodak Information Center** (☎ 800/242–2424). *Kodak Guide to Shooting Great Travel Pictures,* available in bookstores or from Fodor's Travel Publications (☎ 800/533–6478; $16.50 plus $4 shipping).

VIDEOS

Note that the N-PAL video system is used in Argentina, whereas the NTSC system is used in the United States.

CAR TRAVEL

Avenida General Paz completely encircles Buenos Aires. If you're driving into the city from the exterior, you'll know you're in Buenos Aires proper once you've crossed this road. If you're entering the city from the north, chances are you will be on the Ruta Panamericana, one of the country's newest and nicest highways. Autopista 25 de Mayo leads out of the city center toward the airport. R2, which is often under construction, goes between Buenos Aires and the beach resorts in and around Mar del Plata.

CAR RENTAL

Drivers in Buenos Aires move with verve and independence—and with a general disdain for traffic rules. If you want to try your hand at dealing with Argentine road rage, you can rent a car at one of a number of tourist-friendly companies. Annie Millet is recommended, as is Primer Mundo, which is smaller but offers excellent service and better prices. Renting a car in Argentina is expensive ($95 per day for a medium-size car, $475–$600 per week), but having a car gives you much more flexibility. Ask about special rates; generally a better price can be negotiated.

If a car rental company has a branch in another town, arrangements can generally be made for a one-way drop off. Offices in Buenos Aires can make reservations in other locations; provincial government tourist offices also have information on car rental agencies.

A more convenient and comfortable option is to have your travel agent or hotel arrange for a car with a driver (known as a *remise*). This service costs about $20–$25 per hour, sometimes with a three-hour minimum and an additional charge per kilometer if you drive outside the city limits. In smaller towns, the rate is often much less (perhaps $20–$25 for the entire day). Note that when traveling by remise between two cities, it's always cheaper to get a remise from the more rural city. Remises usually end up being quite a bit cheaper than cabs for long rides and are at least marginally cheaper for rides within the city. You have to pay cash—but you'll often spend less than you would for a rental car.

➤ CAR RENTAL AGENCIES: **Alamo** (☎ 800/522–9696 in the U.S.; 0181/759–6200 in the U.K.). **Annie Millet** (✉ Paraguay 1122, Buenos Aires, ☎ 11/4816–8001, FAX 11/4815–6899). **Avis** (✉ Ezeiza Airport, ☎ 11/4480–9387; ✉ Jorge Newberry Airport, ☎ 11/4776–3003; ✉ Cerrito 1527, ☎ 11/4326–5542 or 800/4445–6284 in Buenos Aires; 800/331–1084 in the U.S.; 800/879–2847 in Canada; 02/9353–9000 in Australia; and 09/525–1982 in New Zealand). **Budget** (✉ Av. Santa Fe 11527, ☎ 11/4311–9870 in Buenos Aires; 800/527–0700 in the U.S.; 0144/227–6266 in the U.K.). **Dollar** (☎ 800/800–6000 in the U.S.; 0181/897–0811 in the U.K., where it is known as

Eurodollar; 02/9223–1444 in Australia). **Hertz** (☎ 800/654–3001 in the U.S.; 800/263–0600 in Canada; 0181/897–2072 in the U.K.; 02/9669–2444 in Australia; 03/358–6777 in New Zealand). **Primer Mundo** (✉ Av. Libertador 6553 Buenos Aires, ☎ 11/4787–2140). **Thrifty** (✉ Leandro N. Alem 699 Buenos Aires, ☎ 11/4315–0777).

➤ REMISE SERVICE: **Mitre Remises** (✉ General Roca 1510, Vincente Lopez, ☎ 11/4796–2829 or 11/4794–7228). **Movicar** (☎ 11/4815–1585). **Remises Plaza de Mayo** (✉ Azopardo 523, ☎ 11/4331–4705). **Remise Rioja** (✉ Olivos 2286, ☎ 11/4794–4677 or 11/4794–7228). **Remises Universal** (✉ 25 de Mayo 611, 4th floor, ☎ 11/4315–6555).

PARKING

Parking has been privatized in Buenos Aires, so ticket-happy entrepreneurs are busy putting yellow-metal boots on the front wheels of cars that stand too long at a meter and towing violators off to nearby parking lots. Fines start at $75. There are a few public underground parking garages and numerous private garages, which start at $2–$3 for the first hour and are typically $1.50 per hour thereafter. Most shopping malls have parking garages, which are usually free or give you a reduced rate with a purchase.

CUTTING COSTS

For car rentals in Argentina, it doesn't necessarily cut costs to book before you leave home. But you should reserve ahead if you plan to rent during a holiday period, when vehicles may be in short supply. If you're willing to wait, you can probably get the best rate by renting upon arrival, particularly from a smaller, local company.

Do **look into wholesalers,** companies that do not own fleets but rent in bulk from those that do and often offer better rates than traditional car-rental operations. Payment must be made before you leave home.

➤ WHOLESALERS: **Auto Europe** (☎ 207/842–2000 or 800/223–5555, ℻ 800/235–6321).

INSURANCE

When driving a rented car you are generally responsible for any damage to or loss of the vehicle as well as for any property damage or personal injury that you may cause. Before you rent **see what coverage your personal auto-insurance policy and credit cards already provide** and try to obtain the broadest coverage possible before your arrival in Argentina. Argentine car insurance prices are often significantly higher than in the United States, and the industry has only recently become truly regulated.

REQUIREMENTS & RESTRICTIONS

In Argentina, **your own driver's license is acceptable,** though an International Driver's Permit, available from the American or Canadian Automobile Association, is always a good idea. The minimum driving age is 18, and unlike in some other areas in Latin America, this is enforced via road blocks and spot checks.

AUTO CLUBS

The Automovil Club Argentino operates gas stations, motels, and campgrounds; sends tow trucks and mechanics in case of breakdowns; and provides detailed maps and expert advice (often in English). If you rent a car, the ACA can help you plan your itinerary, give you gas coupons, and make accommodations arrangements. Bring your auto club membership card (The Automovil Club Argentino will usually recognize your local auto-club card) for free advice and discounts.

➤ IN ARGENTINA: **Automovil Club Argentino** (ACA, ✉ Av. del Libertador 1850, ☎ 11/4802–6061).

➤ IN AUSTRALIA: **Australian Automobile Association** (☎ 02/6247–7311).

➤ IN CANADA: **Canadian Automobile Association** (CAA, ☎ 613/247–0117).

➤ IN NEW ZEALAND: **New Zealand Automobile Association** (☎ 09/377–4660).

➤ IN THE U.K.: **Automobile Association** (AA, ☎ 0990/500–600). **Royal Automobile Club** (RAC, ☎ 0990/722–722 for membership; 0345/121–345 for insurance).

➤ IN THE U.S.: **American Automobile Association** (☎ 800/564–6222).

GASOLINE

Gas stations are easy to find in Buenos Aires and other cities and along the highway outside major cities. Farther along the highway and in rural areas, locating a gas station is hit or miss; **don't let your tank get too low.**

Gas is expensive (at least $1 per liter, or about $4 per gallon). There are no regulations on leaded versus unleaded gas and most consumers choose the cheaper, leaded option. Many vehicles also use diesel.

INTERNATIONAL TRAVEL

Paved highways run from Argentina to the Chilean, Bolivian, Paraguayan, and Brazilian borders. It's unlikely, however, that you would enter Argentina by car from another country. If you do, you'll be stopped at the border, asked for your passport, your visa, and any documents you may have about ownership of the car. It's also common for cars and bags to be searched.

ROAD CONDITIONS

Ultramodern multilane highways exist in Argentina, but typically immediately surrounding the major cities. Gradually these highways become narrower routes, and then county roads. Many of these rural roads are not divided and not in particularly good condition.

Highways have been privatized, so you must pay tolls on many more roads. Tolls come frequently and can be steep (one toll, for instance, on the five-hour drive between Buenos Aires and Mar del Plata is $13).

Night driving can be hazardous, as highways and routes typically cut through the center of towns. Cattle often get onto the roads and trucks seldom have all their lights working.

ROAD MAPS
The ACA (☞ Auto Clubs, *above*) has the best road maps of Argentina.

RULES OF THE ROAD
Some common-sense rules of the road: Plan your daily driving distances conservatively. **Don't drive after dark.** Ask before you leave about gas station locations. Obey speed limits (given in kilometers per hour) and traffic regulations. And above all, if you get a traffic ticket, don't argue—it's generally not worth it. In the not so distant past, Argentina was a military state, and the police are still treated as though they wield quite a bit of power. Although you'll see

Argentines offering cash on the spot to avoid getting a written ticket, this is probably not a good idea.

Seat belts are required by law but are not often used; it's a good idea, however, to wear one (if the car has them) as accidents are very common. Turning left on avenues is prohibited unless there's a traffic-light arrow showing that it's okay. Note that **traffic lights are not always observed, so you should proceed with care.** Also note that traffic lights not only turn yellow when they are about to turn red, but also when they are about to turn green. In Buenos Aires, give everyone else on the road priority, especially aggressive colectivo and taxi drivers who think they're race-car drivers.

In towns and cities, a 40 kph (25 mph) speed limit applies on streets, and a 60 kph (37 mph) limit is in effect on avenues. On expressways the limit is 120 kph (75 mph), and on other roads and highways out of town it's 80 kph (50 mph), although this is rarely enforced.

CHILDREN IN ARGENTINA
Argentines generally adore children, and having yours along may prove to be your ticket to meeting locals. Many Argentines prefer to take their children along for a late evening out rather than leave them with a babysitter. As a result, **children are welcome at restaurants;**

it's not uncommon to see youngsters eating midnight dinners with their parents.

FLYING

If your children are two or older **ask about children's airfares.** As a general rule, infants under two not occupying a seat fly at greatly reduced fares or even for free. When booking **confirm carry-on allowances** if you're traveling with infants. In general, for babies charged 10% of the adult fare, you are allowed one carry-on bag and a collapsible stroller; if the flight is full the stroller may have to be checked or you may be limited to less.

Experts agree that it's a good idea to use safety seats aloft for children weighing less than 40 pounds. Airlines set their own policies: U.S. carriers usually require that the child be ticketed, even if he or she is young enough to ride free, since the seats must be strapped into regular seats. Do **check your airline's policy about using safety seats during takeoff and landing.** And since safety seats are not allowed just everywhere in the plane, get your seat assignments early.

When reserving, **request children's meals or a freestanding bassinet** if you need them. But note that bulkhead seats, where you must sit to use the bassinet, may lack an overhead bin or storage space on the floor.

LODGING

Most hotels in Argentina allow children under a certain age to stay in their parents' room at no extra charge, but others charge for them as extra adults; be sure to **find out the cutoff age for children's discounts.**

SIGHTS & ATTRACTIONS

On weekends, Argentine families can be found in droves on day-long outings to the mall, the zoo, or other child-friendly sights. Places that are especially good for children are indicated by a rubber duckie icon in the margin.

SUPPLIES & EQUIPMENT

It's a good idea to **bring books from home,** as literature for children in English is hard to find in Argentina. If you're traveling outside Buenos Aires, you may want to stock up beforehand on items that you're familiar with, such as disposable diapers and baby food.

TRANSPORTATION

If you are renting a car don't forget to **arrange for a car seat** when you reserve.

COMPUTERS ON THE ROAD

You are supposed to declare your computer upon arrival and pay a tax, though this isn't always the case. However, if you're going to be in Argentina for any extended period of time and plan to get Internet access, declare your computer at customs when you enter the country—you'll need to produce either the document from customs or a receipt to get service. If you've declared your computer on the way in, be sure to declare it on the way out also (hold onto the receipt for this purpose as well).

CONSUMER PROTECTION

Whenever shopping or buying travel services in Argentina, **pay with a major credit card** so you can cancel payment or get reimbursed if there's a problem. If you're doing business with a particular company for the first time, **contact your local Better Business Bureau and the attorney general's offices** in your state and the company's home state, as well. Have any complaints been filed? Finally, if you're buying a package or tour, always **consider travel insurance** that includes default coverage (☞ Insurance, *below*).

➤ BBBs: Council of Better Business Bureaus (✉ 4200 Wilson Blvd., Suite 800, Arlington, VA 22203, ☎ 703/276–0100, ℻ 703/525–8277).

CUSTOMS & DUTIES

When shopping, **keep receipts** for all purchases. Upon reentering your country, **be ready to show customs officials what you've bought.** If you feel a duty is incorrect or object to the way your clearance was handled, note the inspector's badge number and ask to see a supervisor. If the problem isn't resolved, write to the appropriate authorities, beginning with the port director at your point of entry.

IN ARGENTINA

If you come directly to Buenos Aires by air or ship, you'll find that customs officials usually wave you through without any inspection. Also, the international airports have introduced a customs system for those with "nothing to declare," which has streamlined the arrival process. Bus passengers usually have their suitcases opened.

Personal clothing and belongings are admitted free of duty, provided they have been used, as are personal jewelry and professional equipment. You are supposed to declare your computer and pay a tax on it. Fishing gear presents no problems. Up to 2 liters of alcoholic beverages, 400 cigarettes, and 50 cigars are admitted duty-free.

Note that **you must pay a $20 departure tax upon leaving the country.**

IN AUSTRALIA

Australia residents who are 18 or older may bring home $A400 worth of souvenirs and gifts (including jewelry), 250 cigarettes or 250 grams of tobacco, and 1,125 ml of alcohol (including wine, beer, and spirits). Residents under 18 may bring back $A200 worth of goods. Prohibited items include meat products. Seeds, plants, and fruits need to be declared upon arrival.

➤ INFORMATION: **Australian Customs Service** (Regional Director, ✉ Box 8, Sydney, NSW 2001, ☎ 02/9213–2000, FAX 02/9213–4000).

IN CANADA

Canadian residents who have been out of Canada for at least seven days may bring home C$500 worth of goods duty-free. If you've been away less than seven days but more than 48 hours, the duty-free allowance drops to C$200; if your trip lasts 24–48 hours, the allowance is C$50. You may not pool allowances with family members. Goods claimed under the C$500 exemption may follow you by mail; those claimed under the lesser exemptions must accompany you. Alcohol and tobacco products may be included in the seven-day and 48-hour exemptions but not in the 24-hour exemption. If you meet the age requirements of the province or territory through which you reenter Canada, you may bring in, duty-free, 1.14 liters (40 imperial ounces) of wine or liquor *or* 24 12-ounce cans or bottles of beer or ale. If you are 16 or older you may bring in, duty-free, 200 cigarettes and 50 cigars. Check ahead of time with Revenue Canada or the Department of Agriculture for policies regarding meat products, seeds, plants, and fruits.

You may send an unlimited number of gifts worth up to C$60 each duty-free to Canada. Label the package UNSOLICITED GIFT—VALUE UNDER $60. Alcohol and tobacco are excluded.

➤ INFORMATION: **Revenue Canada** (✉ 2265 St. Laurent Blvd. S, Ottawa, Ontario K1G 4K3, ☎ 613/993–0534; 800/461–9999 in Canada).

IN NEW ZEALAND

Homeward-bound residents 17 or older may bring back $700 worth of souvenirs and gifts. Your duty-free allowance also includes 4.5 liters of wine or beer; one 1,125-ml bottle of spirits; and either 200 cigarettes, 250 grams of tobacco, 50 cigars, or a combination of the three up to 250 grams. Prohibited items include meat products, seeds, plants, and fruits.

➤ INFORMATION: **New Zealand Customs** (Custom House, ✉ 50 Anzac Ave., Box 29, Auckland, New Zealand, ☎ 09/359–6655, FAX 09/359–6732).

IN THE U.K.

From countries outside the EU, including Argentina, you may bring home, duty-free, 200 cigarettes or 50 cigars; 1 liter of spirits or 2 liters of fortified or sparkling wine or liqueurs; 2 liters of still table wine; 60 ml of perfume; 250 ml of toilet water; plus £136 worth of other goods, including gifts and souvenirs. If returning from outside the EU, prohibited items include meat products, seeds, plants, and fruits.

➤ INFORMATION: **HM Customs and Excise** (✉ Dorset House, Stamford St., Bromley Kent BR1 1XX, ☎ 0171/202–4227).

IN THE U.S.

U.S. residents who have been out of the country for at least 48 hours (and who have not used the $400 allowance or any part of it in the past 30 days) may bring home $400 worth of foreign goods duty-free.

U.S. residents 21 and older may bring back 1 liter of alcohol duty-free. In addition, regardless of your age, you are allowed 200 cigarettes and 100 non-Cuban cigars. Antiques, which the U.S. Customs Service defines as objects more than 100 years old, enter duty-free, as do original works of art done entirely by hand, including paintings, drawings, and sculptures.

You may also send packages home duty-free: up to $200 worth of goods for personal use, with a limit of one parcel per addressee per day (and no alcohol or tobacco products or perfume worth more than $5); label the package PERSONAL USE and attach a list of its contents and their retail value. Do not label the package UNSOLICITED GIFT or your duty-free exemption will drop to $100. Mailed items do not affect your duty-free allowance on your return.

➤ INFORMATION: **U.S. Customs Service** (inquiries, ✉ 1300 Pennsylvania Ave. NW, Washington, DC 20229, ☎ 202/927–6724; complaints, ✉ Office of Regulations and Rulings, 1300 Pennsylvania Ave. NW, Washington, DC 20229; registration of equipment, ✉ Resource Management, 1300 Pennsylvania Ave. NW, Washington, DC 20229, ☎ 202/927–0540).

DINING

The restaurants we list (indicated by ✕) are the cream of the crop in each price category.

MEALS & SPECIALTIES

Meat is still the center of Argentine cuisine. *Asado* (barbeque) is both a style of grilled meat and an event. If you eat at an asado restaurant, are invited to an asado, or go to one at an *estancia* (ranch), be prepared for countless courses of meat, interrupted only by the pouring of wine. *Parrillas* (grills) are also common and are great for casual Argentine fare. All this meat is usually accompanied by a salad and red wine. Pasta (often homemade) and pizza are also frequently available. For more about food in Buenos Aires, *see* Chapter 3.

MEALTIMES

Breakfast is usually served until 10 AM; lunch runs from 12:30 to

2:30; dinner is from 9 to midnight. Several restaurants in Buenos Aires and other large cities stay open all night, or at least well into the morning, catering to the after-theater and nightclub crowd.

RESERVATIONS & DRESS

Reservations are always a good idea; we mention them only when they're essential or are not accepted. Book as far ahead as you can, and reconfirm as soon as you arrive.

Jacket and tie are suggested for evening dining at more formal restaurants in the top price category, but casual chic or informal dress is acceptable at most restaurants. Daytime clothing should be fashionable and on the conservative side. Dress is mentioned in reviews only when men are required to wear a jacket and tie.

DISABILITIES & ACCESSIBILITY

Although international chain hotels in large cities have some suitable rooms, and it's easy to hire private cars with drivers for excursions, Argentina is not well equipped to handle travelers with disabilities. On only a few streets in Buenos Aires, for instance, are there ramps and curb cuts. It takes effort and planning to negotiate museums and other buildings (many have steps that are unfortunately almost entirely unnegotiable with a wheelchair), and to explore the countryside.

➤ COMPLAINTS: **Disability Rights Section** (✉ U.S. Department of Justice, Civil Rights Division, Box 66738, Washington, DC 20035-6738, ☎ 202/514–0301 or 800/514–0301; TTY 202/514–0301 or 800/514–0301; FAX 202/307–1198) for general complaints. **Aviation Consumer Protection Division** (☞ Air Travel, *above*) for airline-related problems. **Civil Rights Office** (✉ U.S. Department of Transportation, Departmental Office of Civil Rights, S-30, 400 7th St. SW, Room 10215, Washington, DC 20590, ☎ 202/366–4648, FAX 202/366–9371) for problems with surface transportation.

LODGING

When discussing accessibility with an operator or reservations agent **ask hard questions.** Are there any stairs, inside *or* out? Are there grab bars next to the toilet *and* in the shower/tub? How wide is the doorway to the room? To the bathroom? For the most extensive facilities meeting the latest legal specifications **opt for newer accommodations.**

TRAVEL AGENCIES

In the United States, although the Americans with Disabilities Act requires that travel firms serve the needs of all travelers, some agencies specialize in working with people with disabilities.

➤ TRAVELERS WITH MOBILITY PROBLEMS: **Access Adventures** (✉ 206 Chestnut Ridge Rd.,

Rochester, NY 14624, ☎ 716/889–9096) is run by a former physical-rehabilitation counselor. **CareVacations** (✉ 5-5110 50th Ave., Leduc, Alberta T9E 6V4, ☎ 780/986–6404 or 780/986–8332) has group tours and is especially helpful with cruise vacations. **Flying Wheels Travel** (✉ 143 W. Bridge St., Box 382, Owatonna, MN 55060, ☎ 507/451–5005 or 800/535–6790, FAX 507/451–1685). **Hinsdale Travel Service** (✉ 201 E. Ogden Ave., Suite 100, Hinsdale, IL 60521, ☎ 630/325–1335).

DISCOUNTS & DEALS

Be a smart shopper and **compare all your options** before making decisions. A plane ticket bought with a promotional coupon from travel clubs, coupon books, and direct-mail offers may not be cheaper than the least expensive fare from a discount ticket agency. And always keep in mind that what you get is just as important as what you save.

Note that **most museums are free one morning or afternoon per week** and that movies are often half price on Wednesday.

DISCOUNT RESERVATIONS

To save money **look into discount-reservations services** with toll-free numbers, which use their buying power to get a better price on hotels, airline tickets, even car rentals. When booking a room, always **call the hotel's local toll-free**

number (if one is available) rather than the central reservations number—you'll often get a better price. Always ask about special packages or corporate rates.

When shopping for the best deal on hotels and car rentals **look for guaranteed exchange rates,** which protect you against a falling dollar. With your rate locked in, you won't pay more, even if the price goes up in the local currency.

The Automovil Club Argentino, the Argentine version of the AAA, will usually recognize AAA cards for discounts within Argentina.

➤ AIRLINE TICKETS: ☎ 800/FLY-4–LESS.

➤ HOTEL ROOMS: **Steigenberger Reservation Service** (☎ 800/223–5652).

PACKAGE DEALS

Don't confuse packages and guided tours. When you buy a package, you travel on your own, just as though you had planned the trip yourself. Fly/drive packages, which combine airfare and car rental, are often a good deal.

ELECTRICITY

To use your U.S.-purchased electric-powered equipment, **bring a converter and adapter.** The current in Argentina is 220 volts, 50 cycles alternating current (AC); wall outlets usually take Continental-type plugs, with two round prongs.

If your appliances are dual-voltage you'll need only an adapter. Don't use 110-volt outlets, marked FOR SHAVERS ONLY, for high-wattage appliances such as blow-dryers. Most laptops operate equally well on 110 and 220 volts and so require only an adapter.

EMBASSIES AND CONSULATES

Besides providing assistance, each of the following embassies also hosts a Thursday evening cocktail party (call any embassy to find out the location of the next event).

➤ AUSTRALIA: ✉ Villanueva 1400, Buenos Aires, ☎ 11/4777–6580.

➤ CANADA: ✉ Tagle 2828, Buenos Aires, ☎ 11/4805–3032.

➤ IRELAND: ✉ Suipacha 1280, 2nd floor, ☎ 11/4325–8588.

➤ NEW ZEALAND: ✉ Echeverria 2140, Buenos Aires, ☎ 11/4787–0593.

➤ SOUTH AFRICA: ✉ Marcelo T. de Alvear 590, Buenos Aires, ☎ 11/4317–2900.

➤ UNITED KINGDOM: ✉ Luis Agote 2412, Buenos Aires, ☎ 11/4803–6021.

➤ UNITED STATES: ✉ Colombia 4300, Buenos Aires, ☎ 11/4777–4533.

EMERGENCIES

All over the area you can call the same numbers in case of emergencies. Each place also has local emergency numbers (☞ Health, *below*).

There's a pharmacy (*farmacia*) on nearly every block in Buenos Aires. Your hotel will be able to guide you to the nearest one. Local pharmacies take turns staying open 24 hours; so at any time of day, you can go to the pharmacy nearest your hotel, and if it's closed, there will be a sign indicating what pharmacy is open.

➤ CONTACTS: **Ambulance** (☎ 107). **Fire** (☎ 1100). **Hospital** (British Hospital, ✉ Perdriel 74, ☎ 11/4304–1081). **Police** (☎ 101 or 11/4383–1111).

ENGLISH-LANGUAGE MEDIA

The best source of information in English is the *Buenos Aires Herald*. It can be purchased at any kiosk throughout the city, for $1 on weekdays and for $1.50 on Sunday. Kioskos on Calle Florida and in front of the Alvear Hotel sell international newspapers, including the *International Herald Tribune,* the *New York Times,* the *Financial Times,* and the *Wall Street Journal.* However, these newspapers are always supplied three days after press date and are always expensive. Most bookstores sell an overpriced and very limited selection of English-language material.

GAY & LESBIAN TRAVEL

In many parts of Buenos Aires, particularly Rosario, gay and lesbian couples mingle with the crowd, relatively unnoticed. However, in more traditional neighborhoods of Buenos Aires, and in smaller towns and rural areas, people are often far less open-minded.

➤ GAY- AND LESBIAN-FRIENDLY TRAVEL AGENCIES: **Different Roads Travel** (✉ 8383 Wilshire Blvd., Suite 902, Beverly Hills, CA 90211, ☎ 323/651–5557 or 800/429–8747, FAX 323/651–3678). **Kennedy Travel** (✉ 314 Jericho Tpk., Floral Park, NY 11001, ☎ 516/352–4888 or 800/237–7433, FAX 516/354–8849). **Now Voyager** (✉ 4406 18th St., San Francisco, CA 94114, ☎ 415/626–1169 or 800/255–6951, FAX 415/626–8626). **Yellowbrick Road** (✉ 1500 W. Balmoral Ave., Chicago, IL 60640, ☎ 773/561–1800 or 800/642–2488, FAX 773/561–4497). **Skylink Travel and Tour** (✉ 1006 Mendocino Ave., Santa Rosa, CA 95401, ☎ 707/546–9888 or 800/225–5759, FAX 707/546–9891), serving lesbian travelers.

HEALTH

FOOD & DRINK

Drinking tap water and eating uncooked greens is considered safe in Buenos Aires. However, if you've got just two weeks, you don't want to waste a minute of it in your hotel room, so be scrupulously careful about what you eat and drink—on as well as off the beaten path. If you have any doubt at all, drink bottled water. The water may be fine, but you have a greater chance of running into contamination outside metropolitan Buenos Aires.

Each year there are several hundred cases of cholera in the northern part of Argentina, mostly in the indigenous communities near the Bolivian border; your best protection is to avoid raw seafood.

MEDICAL SERVICE

Medical service is generally quite adequate and readily accessible in Buenos Aires. It's also free for basic services at public hospitals, though private clinics are usually not nearly as expensive as in the United States.

No one plans to get sick while traveling, but it happens, so **consider signing up with a medical-assistance company.** Members get doctor referrals, emergency evacuation or repatriation, hot lines for medical consultation, cash for emergencies, and other assistance.

➤ MEDICAL-ASSISTANCE COMPANIES: **International SOS Assistance** (✉ 8 Neshaminy Interplex, Suite 207, Trevose, PA 19053, ☎ 215/245–4707 or 800/523–6586, FAX 215/244–9617; ✉ 12 Chemin Riantbosson, 1217 Meyrin 1, Geneva, Switzerland, ☎ 4122/785–6464, FAX 4122/785–6424; ✉ 331 N. Bridge Rd., 17-00, Odeon Towers, Singapore 188720, ☎ 65/338–7800, FAX 65/338–7611).

SHOTS & MEDICATIONS

No specific vaccinations are required for travel to Argentina. According to the Centers for Disease Control (CDC), however, there's a limited risk of cholera, hepatitis B, and dengue. If you plan to visit remote regions or stay for more than six weeks, **check with the CDC's International Travelers Hot Line.** In areas with malaria (in Argentina, you are at risk for malaria only in northern rural areas bordering Bolivia and Paraguay) and dengue, which are both carried by mosquitoes, take mosquito nets, wear clothing that covers the body, apply repellent containing DEET, and use a spray against flying insects in living and sleeping areas. The hot line recommends chloroquine (analen) as an antimalarial agent; no vaccine exists against dengue.

Children (and adults) traveling to Argentina should have current inoculations against measles, mumps, rubella, and polio.

A major health risk is Montezuma's Revenge, or traveler's diarrhea, caused by eating unfamiliar foods or contaminated fruit or vegetables or drinking contaminated water. Mild cases may respond to Imodium (known generically as loperamide) or Pepto-Bismol (not as strong), both of which can be purchased over the counter; paregoric, another antidiarrheal agent, does not require a doctor's prescription in Argentina. Drink plenty of purified water or tea—chamomile is a good folk remedy. In severe cases, rehydrate yourself with a salt–sugar solution (½ teaspoon salt and 4 tablespoons sugar per quart of water).

Note that many medications that require a prescription in the United States and elsewhere, such as antibiotics, are available over the counter in Argentina.

➤ HEALTH WARNINGS: **National Centers for Disease Control** (CDC, National Center for Infectious Diseases, Division of Quarantine, Traveler's Health Section, ✉ 1600 Clifton Rd. NE, M/S E-03, Atlanta, GA 30333, ☎ 888/232–3228, FAX 888/232–3299, www.cdc.gov).

HOLIDAYS

Dates for 2000: New Year's Day (Jan. 1); Labor Day (May 1); Anniversary of the 1810 Revolution (May 25); National Sovereignty Day (June 10); Flag Day (June 20); Independence Day (July 9); Anniversary of San Martín's Death (Aug. 17); Columbus Day (Oct. 9); and Christmas (Dec. 25).

INSURANCE

The most useful travel insurance plan is a comprehensive policy that includes coverage for trip cancellation and interruption, default, trip delay, and medical expenses (with a waiver for preexisting conditions).

Without insurance you will lose all or most of your money if you cancel your trip, regardless of the reason. Default insurance covers you if your tour operator, airline, or cruise line goes out of business. Trip-delay covers expenses that arise because of bad weather or mechanical delays. Study the fine print when comparing policies.

If you're traveling internationally, a key component of travel insurance is coverage for medical bills incurred if you get sick on the road. Such expenses are not generally covered by Medicare or private policies. U.K. residents can buy a travel-insurance policy valid for most vacations taken during the year in which it's purchased (but check pre-existing-condition coverage). British and Australian citizens need extra medical coverage when traveling overseas.

Always **buy travel policies directly from the insurance company**; if you buy it from a cruise line, airline, or tour operator that goes out of business you probably will not be covered for the agency or operator's default, a major risk. Before you make any purchase **review your existing health and home-owner's policies** to find what they cover away from home.

➤ TRAVEL INSURERS: In the United States **Access America** (✉ 6600 W. Broad St., Richmond, VA 23230, ☎ 804/285–3300 or 800/284–8300), **Travel Guard International** (✉ 1145 Clark St., Stevens Point, WI 54481, ☎ 715/345–0505 or 800/826–1300). In Canada **Voyager Insurance** (✉ 44 Peel Center Dr., Brampton, Ontario L6T 4M8, ☎ 905/791–8700; 800/668–4342 in Canada).

➤ INSURANCE INFORMATION: In the United Kingdom the **Association of British Insurers** (✉ 51–55 Gresham St., London EC2V 7HQ, ☎ 0171/600–3333, FAX 0171/696–8999). In Australia the **Insurance Council of Australia** (☎ 03/9614–1077, FAX 03/9614–7924).

THE INTERNET

You can access the Internet in Buenos Aires through your hotel or a Telefonica or Telecom phone office. Internet cafés are not common; occasionally some new ones open, but they don't seem to have much luck.

➤ INTERNET CAFÉS: **Cyber Express** (✉ Florida 482, ☎ 11/4325–0935). **Dos H's Bar** (✉ Viamonte 636, ☎ 11/4326–0878).

LANGUAGE

Argentines speak Spanish (commonly referred to as Castellano). There are a few important differences between Argentine Spanish and that of the rest of Latin America. For example, the informal *tu* form is replaced by *vos* (with some different conjugations). Also, the double L found in words like *pollo* is pronounced with a J-sound rather than a Y-sound.

English replaced French as the country's second language in the 1960s, although most people still have a very limited knowledge of it. Luckily, many hotels, restaurants, and shops employ someone who speaks English.

LANGUAGE SCHOOLS

A wide selection of language courses can be found in the classifieds of Argentina's English-language daily newspaper, the *Buenos Aires Herald*. The list includes schools as well as a large selection of private tutors.

If you you prefer to arrange your Spanish classes prior to your arrival in Argentina, try the Instituto de Lengua Española para Extranjeros (ILEE), which specializes in teaching Spanish to foreigners and has classes beginning every week. The school can help you find a place to stay.

➤ INFORMATION: **Instituto de Lengua Española para Extranjeros** (ILEE, ✉ Lavalle 1619, 7th floor, Unit C, and 4th floor, Unit A, Buenos Aires, ☎ FAX 11/4375–0730).

SPANISH FOR TRAVELERS

A phrase book and language-tape set can help get you started.

➤ PHRASE BOOKS & LANGUAGE-TAPE SETS: *Fodor's Spanish for Travelers* (☎ 800/733–3000 in the U.S.; 800/668–4247 in Canada;

$7 for phrasebook, $16.95 for audio set).

LODGING

The lodgings we list (indicated by 🏨) are the cream of the crop in each price category. We always list the facilities that are available—but we don't specify whether they cost extra: when pricing accommodations, always ask what's included and what costs extra.

Assume that hotels operate on the European Plan (**EP**, with no meals) unless we specify that they use the Continental Plan (**CP**, with a Continental breakfast daily), Breakfast Plan (**BP**, with a full breakfast daily), Modified American Plan (**MAP**, with breakfast and dinner daily), or are all-inclusive (including all meals and most activities).

ALBERGUES TRANSITORIOS

Albergues transitorios (temporary lodgings) is the euphemistic name for drive-in hotels, which are generally used for romantic trysts. Very common in this country where people often live with their parents until marriage, they are easily recognizable by their hourly rates and purple and orange exterior lights.

Real motels can be found through the Automovil Club Argentino (☞ Auto Clubs *in* Car Travel, *above*). Generally these motels are inexpensive ($35–$45 a night) and more than adequate.

APARTMENT & VILLA RENTALS

If you want a home base that's roomy enough for a family and comes with cooking facilities **consider a furnished rental.** These can save you money, especially if you're traveling with a group.

➤ INTERNATIONAL AGENT: Hideaways International (✉ 767 Islington St., Portsmouth, NH 03801, ☎ 603/430–4433 or 800/843–4433, FAX 603/430–4444; membership $99).

CAMPING

Campgrounds can be found in popular tourist destinations, including some beach areas. Usually they have running water, electricity, and bathroom facilities with toilets and showers. The **Automovil Club Argentino** (☞ Auto Clubs *in* Car Travel, *above*) can provide a list of campgrounds nationwide. Provincial tourist offices in Buenos Aires have lists of campgrounds in their regions. Some have telephones so that you can make reservations.

HOME EXCHANGES

If you would like to exchange your home for someone else's **join a home-exchange organization,** which will send you its updated listings of available exchanges for a year and will include your own listing in at least one of them. It's up to you to make specific arrangements.

➤ EXCHANGE CLUBS: **HomeLink International** (✉ Box 650, Key West, FL 33041, ☎ 305/294–7766 or 800/638–3841, FAX 305/294–1448; $88 per year). **Intervac U.S.** (✉ Box 590504, San Francisco, CA 94159, ☎ 800/756–4663, FAX 415/435–7440; $83 per year).

HOSTELS

No matter what your age you can **save on lodging costs by staying at hostels.** Hostelling International (HI), the umbrella group for a number of national youth-hostel associations, offers single-sex, dorm-style beds and, at many hostels, couples rooms and family accommodations. Membership in any HI national hostel association, open to travelers of all ages, allows you to stay in HI-affiliated hostels at member rates (about $10–$25 per night). Members also have priority if the hostel is full. Membership in the United States is $25, in Canada C$26.75, in the United Kingdom £9.30, in Australia $44, and in New Zealand $24.

➤ INTERNATIONAL ORGANIZATIONS: **Australian Youth Hostel Association** (✉ 10 Mallett St., Camperdown, NSW 2050, ☎ 02/9565–1699, FAX 02/9565–1325). **Hostelling International— American Youth Hostels** (✉ 733 15th St. NW, Suite 840, Washington, DC 20005, ☎ 202/783–6161, FAX 202/783–6171). **Hostelling International—Canada** (✉ 400–205 Catherine St., Ottawa, Ontario K2P 1C3, ☎ 613/237–7884, FAX 613/237–7868).

Youth Hostel Association of England and Wales (✉ Trevelyan House, 8 St. Stephen's Hill, St. Albans, Hertfordshire AL1 2DY, ☎ 01727/855–215 or 01727/845–047, ℻ 01727/844–126). **Youth Hostels Association of New Zealand** (✉ Box 436, Christchurch, New Zealand, ☎ 03/379–9970, ℻ 03/365–4476).

➤ LOCAL ORGANIZATIONS: **Buenos Aires Hostel** (✉ Av. Brasil 675, Buenos Aires, ☎ 11/4362–9133). **Youth Hostel Association** (✉ Talcahuano 214, 2nd Floor, Buenos Aires, ☎ 11/4372–1001).

HOTELS

Amenities in most nice hotels—private baths, 24-hour room service, heating and air-conditioning, cable TV, dry cleaning, and restaurants—are above average. The less expensive the hotel, the fewer amenities you get, though you can still find charm, cleanliness, and hospitality. You may or may not have television and a phone in your room, though you will find them somewhere in the hotel. Rooms that have a private bath may only have a shower, and in some cases, there will be a shared bath in the hall. In all but the most upscale hotels, you may be asked to leave your key at the reception desk whenever you leave, and many hotels have a curfew, so if you arrive after the reception desk closes, you may not be able to get your key. Most hotels in all categories offer breakfast, whether or not there is a full restaurant in the hotel.

MAIL & SHIPPING

Post offices are found every six or seven blocks or so throughout the city and are typically open weekdays from 9 to 6. Most are also open on Saturday until 1, but often, even if the office is closed, a pleading smile will let you in to mail a letter. Stamps are available at kiosks, but most people go directly to the post office and stand in line to mail a letter, which seems to drastically reduce lost mail.

When delivery is normal and there are no strikes or postal vacations, mail takes 6–15 days to get from Buenos Aires to the United States and 10–15 days to the United Kingdom. Put postcards in envelopes and they will arrive more quickly. An international airmail letter costs $1.

EXPRESS MAIL

International Express services take three to five days for all international destinations, and the cost can be steep (for instance, a letter to the United States via FedEx costs $28). Services available include DHL, Federal Express, and UPS.

➤ COMPANIES: **DHL** (✉ Moreno 631, Buenos Aires, ☎ 11/4347–0600). **Federal Express** (✉ Maipu 753, Buenos Aires, ☎ 11/4630–0300). **UPS** (✉ Bernardo de

Yrigoyen 974, Buenos Aires, ☎ 11/4307–2174).

RECEIVING MAIL

You can receive mail in Buenos Aires at the Correo Central (Central Post Office). Letters should be addressed to Lista/Poste Restante, Correo Central, 1000 Buenos Aires, Argentina. American Express cardholders can have mail sent to American Express.

➤ LOCATIONS: **American Express** (⊠ Arenales 707, 1061 Buenos Aires, ☎ 11/4312–0900). **Buenos Aires Correo Central** (⊠ Sarmiento 151, 1st floor, Buenos Aires, ☎ 11/4311–5030 or 11/4311–5040).

MONEY MATTERS

Prices throughout this guide are given for adults. Substantially reduced fees are almost always available for children, students, and senior citizens. For information on taxes, *see* Taxes, *below*.

ATMS

Before leaving home, **make sure that your credit cards have been programmed for ATM use in Argentina.** Note that Discover is accepted mostly in the United States. Local bank cards often do not work overseas or may access only your checking account; **ask your bank about a MasterCard/Cirrus or Visa debit card,** which works like a bank card but can be used at any ATM displaying a MasterCard/Cirrus or Visa logo. These

cards, too, may tap only your checking account; check with your bank about their policy.

Although fees charged for ATM transactions may be higher, Cirrus and Plus exchange rates are excellent, because they are based on wholesale rates offered only by major banks. ATMs are getting easier to find, especially in Buenos Aires, Cordóba, Mar del Plata, and other major cities and resort towns.

➤ ATM LOCATIONS: **Cirrus** (☎ 800/424–7787). A list of **Plus** locations is available at your local bank.

COSTS

For decades Argentina had one of the most volatile economies in the world, a boom-bust seesaw driven by inflation that sometimes rose several percentage points in a day. For the past few years inflation has been tamed, however, making it more likely that costs can be predicted with some degree of accuracy.

Argentina is not inexpensive, though occasional bargains can be found. The most sumptuous dinners, particularly in French restaurants, can run as high as $100 per person with wine and tip. But a thick slab of rare, wood-grilled sirloin with salad, potatoes, a house wine, and an espresso will cost around $20 at Buenos Aires steak houses.

When ordering drinks, ask for Argentine liquors or you'll be paying for the tremendous import fees. A bottle of the national favorite, Chivas Regal, costs $75–$100 in shops, for instance. Simply ask for *"whiskey nacional, por favor"* or *"vodka nacional."*

Sample Prices: A cup of coffee in a café, $2.50; with milk, $3. A bottle of soda, $1. A taxi ride in central Buenos Aires, $4–$8. A tango show with a couple of drinks, about $60. A double room in a moderately priced, well-situated hotel, including taxes, $100–$130.

CREDIT CARDS

If you choose to bring just one card, Visa is recommended, as it is the most readily accepted. American Express, Diners Club, and MasterCard are the most commonly accepted after Visa. It may be easiest to use your credit card whenever possible—the exchange rate only varies by a fraction of a cent, so you won't need to worry whether your purchase is charged on the day of purchase or at some point in the future. Note, however that you may get a better deal if you pay with cash.

Throughout this guide, the following abbreviations are used: **AE,** American Express; **DC,** Diner's Club; **MC,** MasterCard; and **V,** Visa.

➤ REPORTING LOST CARDS: **American Express** (☎ 11/4312–1661). **Diners Club** (☎ 11/4708–2484).

MasterCard (☎ 11/4331–2555). **Visa** (☎ 11/4379–3333).

CURRENCY

In the past, dramatic value swings occurred during periods of hyperinflation. In fact, during a bleak but brief period, a cup of coffee cost twice as much in local currency after dinner as it did for breakfast. But greater economic stability was achieved in the early 1990s and at press time the currency appeared to be more stable than it had been in the past.

One peso (P) equals 100 centavos. Peso notes are in denominations of P100, 50, 20, 10, 5, and 2. Coins are in denominations of P1, and 50, 25, 10, 5, and 1 centavos.

CURRENCY EXCHANGE

For the past few years, the Argentine peso has been pegged to the U.S. dollar (although it's overvalued and worth less on the international market, the Argentine peso functions interchangeably with the U.S. dollar in Argentina). It's always handy to have pesos with you for the occasions when dollars are not accepted. The amount of pesos you require can usually be obtained by making a purchase with a large U.S. dollar bill and requesting the change in pesos (as pesos and dollars are so often used interchangeably, you can request your change in either currency).

Dollars are frequently accepted throughout Buenos Aires by cab drivers and at restaurants, hotels, and shops; often places that accept dollars will post a sign to say so. Be sure that bills are not torn or dirty; **dollars in poor condition won't be accepted.**

Residents of countries other than the United States are advised to change their currencies to dollars before their journey, as dollars are the easiest to use and exchange. At press time, 1 U.S. dollar equaled 1 peso, 1 Canadian dollar equaled roughly .70 pesos, and 1 pound sterling equaled roughly 1.65 pesos.

You can change money at your hotel, at banks, or at *casas de cambio* (money changers), which offer competitive rates. There's an exchange desk at Buenos Aires's Ezeiza Airport, right near the exit to the parking lot. Pesos can also generally be obtained by making a purchase in dollars and requesting the change in pesos. Exchange fees are better at banks, but not significantly so—and there are lines. Though you'll get a few pesos less by exchanging at your hotel, you'll save yourself time. Plan ahead, since it's often hard to change large amounts of money at hotels on weekends, even in cities.

Even if you do pay for items primarily in dollars, it's a good idea to have some pesos with you. Also, in rural areas, dollars are less likely to be accepted, so you'll want to have pesos. You may not be able to change currency in rural areas at all, so **don't leave the city without adequate amounts of pesos** in small denominations.

➤ BANKS AND EXCHANGE SERVICES: **America** (✉ Sarmiento 501, ☎ 11/4393–0054). **Baires** (✉ San Martín 215, ☎ 11/4325–8547). **Banco Piano** (✉ San Martín 347, ☎ 11/4394–2463). **Chase Manhattan Bank** (✉ Arenales 707, 5th floor, ☎ 11/4319–2400). **Citibank** (✉ Bartolome Mitre 502, ☎ 11/4329–1000). **Forex Cambio** (✉ Marcelo T. de Alvear 540, ☎ 11/4312–7729). **Republic National Bank of New York** (✉ Bartolome Mitre 343, ☎ 11/4349–1600). **Western Union** (✉ Av. Cordoba 917, ☎ 11/4322–7774).

TAXES

Sales tax in Argentina is 21%. The tax is usually included in the price that you see.

TIPPING

In Spanish, tips are called *propinas*. Add 10%–15% in bars and restaurants (10% is enough in a casual café or if the bill runs high). Argentines round off a taxi fare, though some cabbies who frequent hotels popular with tourists seem to expect more. Hotel porters should be tipped at least $1. Also give doormen and ushers about $1. Beauty- and barbershop personnel generally get around 5%.

TRAVELER'S CHECKS

Larger stores in Buenos Aires will occasionally accept traveler's checks, but smaller shops and restaurants are leery of them.

You'll probably have to go to the bank or the American Express office to change your checks.

The benefit of traveler's checks is that lost or stolen checks can usually be replaced within 24 hours. To ensure a speedy refund, buy your own traveler's checks—don't let someone else pay for them: such irregularities as this can cause delays.

PACKING

Argentines in general are very fashion and appearance conscious.

If you're doing business in Argentina, bring the same attire you would wear in U.S. and European cities: for men, suits and ties; for women, suits for day wear and suitable dinner clothes.

For sightseeing and leisure, casual clothing and good walking shoes are desirable and appropriate, although **shorts should be avoided by both men and women,** especially out of the city. In the smaller towns and villages, dress especially conservatively—no short skirts or halters.

Getting dressed up for dinner is not required in most cities, though more than jeans is expected in Buenos Aires.

For beach vacations, bring lightweight sportswear, a bathing suit, a sun hat, and sunscreen. In winter, bring much more. In your carry-on luggage **bring an extra pair of eyeglasses or contact lenses** and **enough of any medication you take** to last the entire trip. You may also want your doctor to write a spare prescription using the drug's generic name, since brand names may vary from country to country. In luggage to be checked, **never pack prescription drugs or valuables.** To avoid customs delays, carry medications in their original packaging. And don't forget to copy down and carry addresses of offices that handle refunds of lost traveler's checks.

Other useful items include a screw-top water bottle, a money pouch, a travel flashlight, extra batteries, a pocketknife with a bottle opener, a medical kit, binoculars, and a pocket calculator to help with currency conversions. Take more film than you ever thought you would use and extra batteries for your camera. If you're traveling with children, take books and games.

CHECKING LUGGAGE

How many carry-on bags you can bring with you is up to the airline. Most allow 2, but not always, so make sure that everything you carry aboard will fit under your seat, and get to the gate early. Note that if you have a seat at the back of the plane, you'll probably board first, while the overhead bins are still empty.

If you are flying internationally, note that baggage allowances may be determined not by piece but by weight—generally 88 pounds (40 kilograms) in first class, 66 pounds (30 kilograms) in business class, and 44 pounds (20 kilograms) in economy.

Airline liability for baggage is limited to $1,250 per person on flights within the United States. On international flights it amounts to $9.07 per pound or $20 per kilogram for checked baggage (roughly $640 per 70-pound bag) and $400 per passenger for unchecked baggage. You can buy additional coverage at check-in for about $10 per $1,000 of coverage, but it excludes a rather extensive list of items, shown on your airline ticket.

Before departure **itemize your bags' contents** and their worth, and label the bags with your name, address, and phone number. (If you use your home address, cover it so that potential thieves can't see it readily.) Inside each bag **pack a copy of your itinerary.** At check-in **make sure that each bag is correctly tagged** with the destination airport's three-letter code. If your bags arrive damaged or fail to arrive at all, file a written report with the airline before leaving the airport.

PASSPORTS & VISAS

It's a good idea to **make two photocopies of your passport** (one for someone at home and another for you, carried separately from your passport). If you lose your passport promptly call the nearest embassy or consulate and the local police.

ENTERING ARGENTINA

U.S., Canadian, and British citizens do not need a visa for visits of up to 90 days, though they must **carry a passport.** Upon entering Argentina, you'll receive a tourist visa stamp on your passport valid for 90 days. If you need to stay longer, exit the country for one night, and upon re-entering Argentina, your passport will be stamped with an additional 90 days. The fine for overstaying your tourist visa is $50, payable upon departure at the airport. If you do overstay your visa, plan to arrive at the airport several hours in advance of your flight so that you have ample time to take care of the fine.

➤ CANADIAN CITIZENS: **Passport Office** (☎ 819/994–3500 or 800/567–6868).

➤ U.K. CITIZENS: **London Passport Office** (☎ 0990/210–410).

➤ U.S. CITIZENS: **National Passport Information Center** (☎ 900/225–5674; calls are 35¢ per minute for automated service, $1.05 per minute for operator service). **Office of Passport Services** (☎ 202/647–0518).

➤ AUSTRALIAN CITIZENS: **Australian Passport Office** (☎ 131–232).

➤ NEW ZEALAND CITIZENS: **New Zealand Passport Office** (☎ 04/494–0700 for information on how to apply; 04/474–8000 or 0800/225–050 in New Zealand for information on applications already submitted).

SAFETY

Buenos Aires is one of the safest cities in the world. At any time of night, you'll see young children and little old ladies strolling around, apparently unconcerned about the hour or the darkness. Police constantly patrol any areas where tourists are likely to be, and violent crime is rare.

Smaller towns and villages in Argentina are even safer, so much so that you may find yourself in a room in a small country inn where the door doesn't have a lock.

That said, keep in mind that there are terrible incidents and crazy people everywhere, and Argentina is no exception. At night, **go out in pairs, or preferably in groups,** and remember that Buenos Aires is the ninth largest city in the world. When in doubt, follow local advice on whether or not it's safe to walk at night and where.

At all times, **keep documents, money, and credit cards hidden in a waist money belt or in zipped pockets.** Don't carry valuables swinging from your shoulder or hanging around your neck. Always **remain alert for pickpockets.** Passports, tickets, and other valuables are best left in hotel safes, when available.

Wear the simplest of watches and **do not wear any jewelry you're not willing to lose**—stories of travelers having chains and even earrings yanked off of them are not uncommon. Keep cameras in a secure camera bag, preferably one with a chain or wire embedded in the strap.

Generally you'll find that the local people are friendly and helpful and that the biggest crime you're likely to encounter is an exorbitantly overpriced gaucho poncho.

WOMEN IN ARGENTINA

Women are safer in Buenos Aires than in many other major cities in the world, but violent crimes still occur. It's best not to over- or underdress, nor to flash jewelry on the street in Buenos Aires or elsewhere. Above all, just act as if you know what you're doing and take normal precautions and you should have no problems.

SENIOR-CITIZEN TRAVEL

Senior citizens are highly revered in Argentina and are generally treated with the greatest of respect. There's no reason that active, well-traveled senior citizens should not visit Argentina, whether on an independent (but prebooked) vacation, an escorted tour, or an adventure vacation. Argentina has plenty of good hotels and competent ground operators who can meet your flights and organize your sightseeing.

To qualify for age-related discounts, **mention your senior-citizen status up front** when booking hotel reservations (not when checking out) and before you're seated in restaurants (not when paying the bill). Note that discounts may be limited to certain menus, days, or hours. When renting a car, ask about promotional car-rental discounts, which can be cheaper than senior-citizen rates.

Before you leave home, however, **determine what medical services your health insurance will cover.** Note that Medicare does not provide for payment of hospital and medical services outside the United States. If you need additional travel insurance, buy it (☞ Insurance, *above*).

➤ EDUCATIONAL PROGRAMS: **Elderhostel** (✉ 75 Federal St., 3rd floor, Boston, MA 02110, ☎ 877/426–8056, 📠 877/426–2166).

SHOPPING

Buenos Aires is a great place to buy clothing, leather goods, and furs. Paintings, engravings, and fine local wine are other good options. In any case, just looking at the displays—of Tierra del Fuego fox in the latest Yves St. Laurent styles, butter-soft leathers, evening gowns with snakeskin appliqués, cashmere sweaters, loafers, boots, briefcases, and bags—can be a window-shopper's delight. Look

for *liquidaciones* (sale) signs in the window. Argentine shops have fixed prices but often give discounts for cash (in the smaller shops, you can often begin a bargaining session by asking, "So, how much is the cash price?").

STUDENTS IN ARGENTINA

To save money, **look into deals available through student-oriented travel agencies.** To qualify you'll need a bona fide student ID card. Members of international student groups are also eligible.

➤ STUDENT IDS & SERVICES: **Council on International Educational Exchange** (CIEE, ✉ 205 E. 42nd St., 14th floor, New York, NY 10017, ☎ 212/822–2600 or 888/268–6245, 📠 212/822–2699) for mail orders only, in the United States. **Travel Cuts** (✉ 187 College St., Toronto, Ontario M5T 1P7, ☎ 416/979–2406 or 800/667–2887) in Canada.

SUBWAY TRAVEL

Buenos Aires's subway system, known as the *subte,* is excellent. It's the oldest in South America, dating from 1913, and many of the stations are decorated with historic scenes of the city or murals by contemporary artists. The subte serves only a small part of the city and does not go anywhere near the suburbs. It was constructed at a time when Buenos Aires consisted of El Centro and La Boca. At that time, Belgrano was a suburb, and anything beyond that was countryside. However, in the last 70 years, Buenos Aires has spread significantly, eating up suburbs and incorporating them into the city far faster than the subway can keep up. But the subway is expanding.

The subte system consists of five lines, which all basically start in El Centro and fan out in different directions. Line A, the oldest and most historic line, runs from Plaza de Mayo to Primera Junta. It's worth a trip on Line A, even if you don't need to travel anywhere, just to see the old wooden subway cars. Line B goes from Línea Alem, which is in the financial district of El Centro, near Puerto Madero, to Federico Lacroze. Line C connects the two major train stations, Retiro and Constitución, making stops along the way in El Centro. Line D runs from Catedral on Plaza de Mayo to Jose Hernández, in Belgrano (a new stop is under construction, and as of January 1, 2000, the final stop on Line D was due to be Juramento, also in Belgrano). Line E goes from Bolívar, a few blocks from Plaza de Mayo, to Plaza de los Virreyes. A new line, to be called Line H, which would wrap around the city, is currently in the planning stage and should be in place by 2002.

At press time, tokens cost about 50¢, but discussions are underway to raise the price. One token is valid for any length trip on the subway. The subway is closed between 10 PM and 5 AM.

TAXIS

Taxis are everywhere in Buenos Aires, so you should never have a problem getting one on the street. Cabs are generally independently owned and operated, and as such, their owners are always on the lookout for business. They are usually safe, but keep in mind that robberies of taxis do occur, especially in areas known to have banks, so be aware. If you don't like the look of a cab, or don't feel comfortable with the driver, do not get in the car. Another cab will be along in a matter of seconds.

Note that hailing a cab involves holding your arm out in a perpendicular fashion, as if you were pointing to something across the street. The traditional New York manner of hailing a cab, with the hand raised up in the air, will flag down a bus in Buenos Aires.

Meters start at $1.20 and increase in small increments per ¼ kilometer. In the central downtown area, fares are about $2–$4; out to Recoleta will cost you $5–$6; San Telmo $4–$6; and Belgrano $8.

TELEPHONES

Public phones are found on nearly every block and usually operate with a telephone card, which can be purchased at any kiosk. Simply slide the card in, wait for the reading of how many minutes you have remaining, and dial the number. Some public phones are coin operated, and a rare few are still operated by an old phone token. To make a long-distance call from a pay phone, go to a telecentro, which are found throughout the city and have private booths and fax services. (Note that you still need a local phone card to make a long-distance call, even if you have your own calling card.)

Using a phone anywhere can be a frustrating experience, despite the privatization of ENTEL, the formerly government-run telephone company. Phone numbers change frequently and it's common to get the message *"equivocado"* ("wrong number"). Often the best bet is to get operator assistance or to have the operator at your hotel help put through your calls. Using phones in telecentros or *locutorios* (telephone offices) is another good option.

COUNTRY & AREA CODES

The country code for Argentina is 54. To call Argentina from overseas, dial the country code (54), and then the area code, omitting the first 0. The area code for Buenos Aires is 11, and all numbers in the city start with 4.

DIRECTORY & OPERATOR INFORMATION

For information, dial 110. For the time, 113. For an international operator, dial 000. For information about international calls, dial 19.

INTERNATIONAL CALLS

Be prepared for a hollow sound or even an echo of your own voice for the first minute or so of an international call. This typically goes away after the first few sentences of a conversation.

Most hotels have international direct dial, but may charge up to $3 per long-distance call. International calls can also be made from telephone company offices around Buenos Aires and at telecentros.

The country code is 1 for the United States and Canada, 61 for Australia, 64 for New Zealand, and 44 for the United Kingdom.

LOCAL CALLS

Hotels charge a per minute rate that can be quite high, even for local calls. Ask the front desk ahead of time about calling; the cost varies depending on whether you are calling at prime time (8 AM–8 PM) or not.

If you need to call the cellular phone number of a resident of Buenos Aires, dial 15 before the number: This is the access code to reach a cellular phone from a non-cellular phone (you don't need to dial this number if you're calling from another cellular phone with a Buenos Aires number). Local cellular phone charges are $1 per call, charged to the caller.

LONG-DISTANCE CALLS

When calling from one area code to another in Argentina, add a 0 before the area code.

Many hotels charge up to $3 per call on top of the regular rate. To make a long-distance call from a public phone, look for a telecentro, which can be found throughout the city and have private telephone cabins as well as fax services. You can use your calling card to make a long-distance call from a pay phone, but you will still need to purchase a local phone card to access a line.

LONG-DISTANCE SERVICES

AT&T, MCI, and Sprint access codes make calling long distance relatively convenient, but you may find the local access number blocked in many hotel rooms or you may be charged a fee to access the number. First ask the hotel operator to connect you. If the hotel operator balks ask for an international operator, or dial the international operator yourself. One way to improve your odds of getting connected to your long-distance carrier is to travel with more than one company's calling card (a hotel may block Sprint, for example, but not MCI). If all else fails call from a pay phone.

➤ ACCESS CODES: For local access numbers abroad, contact AT&T (☎ 800/874–4000), MCI (☎ 800/

444–4444), or **Sprint** (☎ 800/793–1153).

PHONE CARDS

Phone cards are available at kiosks. One card unit buys two or three minutes of time, depending on whether you are calling prime time (8 AM–8 PM) or otherwise.

PUBLIC PHONES

Public phones in Argentina are reliable and are found on nearly every block. They generally operate with a telephone card, which can be purchased at any kiosk. Simply slide the card in, wait for the reading of how many minutes you have remaining, and dial the number. Some public phones are coin operated and a rare few are still operated by old phone tokens.

If you plan to use a calling card at a public phone, you'll still need a local phone card to gain access to a line. To make a long-distance call from a public phone, you're better off finding a telecentro.

TIME

New York is one time zone behind Buenos Aires in summer (it's two in winter, as Argentina does not observe American daylight savings time), and there's only a four-hour difference between Los Angeles and Buenos Aires.

TOURS & PACKAGES

On a prepackaged tour or independent vacation everything is prearranged so you'll spend less time planning—and often get it all at a good price.

BUS TOURS

Buenos Aires Tours organizes extensive bus tours of the city and can help you plan travel all over the country. Cauces Tours arranges bus tours of the city and neighboring suburbs and also arranges travel throughout Argentina.

WALKING TOURS

If you understand Spanish, you can take advantage of the free guided walking tours offered by the Municipalidad. The schedule varies each month (in summer it's closed); details are available from the tourist office (☞ Visitor Information, *below*).

BOOKING WITH AN AGENT

Travel agents are excellent resources. But it's a good idea to collect brochures from several agencies because some agents' suggestions may be influenced by relationships with tour and package firms that reward them for volume sales. If you have a special interest **find an agent with expertise in that area**; ASTA (☞ Travel Agencies, *below*) has a database of specialists worldwide.

Make sure your travel agent knows the accommodations and other services of the place they're recommending. Ask about the hotel's location, room size, beds, and whether it has a pool, room service, or programs for children, if you care about these. Has your agent been there in person or sent others whom you can contact?

Do some homework on your own, too: Local tourism boards can provide information about lesser-known and small-niche operators, some of which may sell only direct.

BUYER BEWARE

Each year consumers are stranded or lose their money when tour operators—even large ones with excellent reputations—go out of business. So **check out the operator.** Ask several travel agents about its reputation, and try to **book with a company that has a consumer-protection program.** (Look for information in the company's brochure.) In the United States, members of the National Tour Association and United States Tour Operators Association are required to set aside funds to cover your payments and travel arrangements in case the company defaults. It's also a good idea to choose a company that participates in the American Society of Travel Agent's Tour Operator Program (TOP); ASTA will act as mediator in any disputes between you and your tour operator.

Remember that the more your package or tour includes the better you can predict the ultimate cost of your vacation. Make sure you know exactly what is covered, and **beware of hidden costs.** Are taxes, tips, and transfers included? Entertainment and excursions? These can add up.

➤ TOUR-OPERATOR RECOMMENDATIONS: **American Society of Travel Agents** (☞ Travel Agencies, *below*). **Buenos Aires Tours** (✉ Lavalle 1444, ☎ 11/4371–2304 or 11/4371–2390). **Cauces Tours** (✉ Maipu 995, ☎ 11/4314–9001). **Municipalidad** (✉ City Hall; Sarmiento 1551, 5th floor, ☎ 11/4372–3612). **National Tour Association** (NTA, ✉ 546 E. Main St., Lexington, KY 40508, ☎ 606/226–4444 or 800/682–8886). **United States Tour Operators Association** (USTOA, ✉ 342 Madison Ave., Suite 1522, New York, NY 10173, ☎ 212/599–6599 or 800/468–7862, 📠 212/599–6744).

TRAIN TRAVEL

Argentina's rail system, which was built by the British, no longer plays an important role in Argentina's transportation system. Trains tend to run rather infrequently and go to few destinations and are often not as comfortable as luxury buses. The most popular routes are all from Buenos Aires to Mar de la Plata and Bariloche. There's also a special tourist-oriented train, the Tren de los Nubes (Train of the Clouds), that goes through the Andes.

Train tickets are inexpensive. Usually there are two classes. Plan to buy your train tickets three days ahead, two weeks in summer months, and arrive at the station well before departure time. Reservations must be made in person at the local train station.

Buenos Aires is served by six private commuter rail lines, which provide extensive service throughout the city proper and the suburbs. The trains run on a surprisingly consistent schedule: every 5–10 minutes during rush hour, with far fewer trains off-peak. You can get train schedules at stations.

Tickets must be purchased before boarding the train. They can be bought from an attendant or, at some stations, through an automatic machine. Fares are based on the point of departure and the destination. In general, fares range from 40¢ for a journey of a few stops to $2 for a trip to the end of the line; the fare for an *ida y vuelta* (round-trip) ticket to Tigre on the Delta is only $1.60.

On some lines there is a more expensive train called the *diferencial,* which is climate controlled and on which you are assured a seat. These usually cost about four times as much as regular trains and run far more infrequently; nonetheless, it may be worth the money and the wait on brutally hot days in January.

Hold onto your ticket: Once on board, a uniformed ticket collector may ask you to show your ticket.

If you do not have your ticket, you will be asked to pay an on-the-spot fine of $3.50–$6.50. And the time it takes to pay the fine could cause you to miss your stop.

➤ COMMUTER TRAIN LINES: **Línea Belgrano** (⊠ Estación Retiro, Av. Ramos Mejía 1430, ☎ 11/4317–4407). **Línea Mitre** (⊠ Estación Retiro, Av. Ramos Mejía 1398, across from Sheraton Hotel, ☎ 11/4317–4445). **Línea Roca** (⊠ Estación Constitución, Av. Brasil 1138, ☎ 11/4304–0038). **Línea San Martín** (⊠ Estación Retiro, Av. Ramos Mejía 1552, ☎ 11/4317–4445). **Línea Sarmiento** (⊠ Estación Once, Bartolomé Mitre 2815, ☎ 11/4861–0043). **Línea Urquiza** (⊠ Estación Lacroze, Av. Federico Lacroze 4181, ☎ 11/4553–0044).

TRAVEL AGENCIES

A good travel agent puts your needs first. Look for an agency that has been in business at least five years, emphasizes customer service, and has someone on staff who specializes in your destination. In addition **make sure the agency belongs to a professional trade organization,** such as ASTA in the United States. If your travel agency is also acting as your tour operator *see* Buyer Beware *in* Tours & Packages, *above.*

➤ AGENT REFERRALS: **American Society of Travel Agents** (ASTA, ☎ 800/965–2782 24-hr hot line, FAX 703/684–8319). **Association of**

British Travel Agents (⊠ 55–57 Newman St., London W1P 4AH, ☎ 0171/637–2444, FAX 0171/637–0713). **Association of Canadian Travel Agents** (⊠ 1729 Bank St., Suite 201, Ottawa, Ontario K1V 7Z5, ☎ 613/521–0474, FAX 613/521–0805). **Australian Federation of Travel Agents** (⊠ Level 3, 309 Pitt St., Sydney 2000, ☎ 02/9264–3299, FAX 02/9264–1085). **Travel Agents' Association of New Zealand** (⊠ Box 1888, Wellington 10033, ☎ 04/499–0104, FAX 04/499–0786).

VISITOR INFORMATION

Information kiosks run by the city along Calle Florida, have English-speaking personnel and city maps, but few brochures. A great place to get friendly tourist advice and tons of brochures, maps, and even vacation-planning tips is at the information counter on the second floor of the Galerías Pacífico shopping center.

You can get information over the phone, on weekdays, 9–5, from the Dirección de Turismo del Gobierno de la Ciudad de Buenos Aires (Tourist Department of the City of Buenos Aires). The Secretaria de Turismo de la Nación, the national tourism office, runs a telephone information service, which is toll free from any point in Argentina, 24 hours a day.

➤ LOCAL CONTACTS: **Dirección de Turismo del Gobierno de la Ciudad de Buenos Aires** (Tourist

Department of the City of Buenos Aires; ☎ 15/4763612). **Secretaria de Turismo de la Nación** (✉ Av. Santa Fe 883, ☎ 11/4312–2232 or 11/4312–5550).

➤ ARGENTINA GOVERNMENT TOURIST OFFICES: **New York** (✉ 12 W. 56th St., New York, NY 10019, ☎ 212/603–0443). **Los Angeles** (✉ 5055 Wilshire Blvd., Los Angeles, CA 90036, ☎ 213/930–0681). **Miami** (✉ 2655 Le Jeune Rd., Miami, FL 33134, ☎ 305/442–1366).

➤ U.S. GOVERNMENT ADVISORIES: **U.S. Department of State** (✉ Overseas Citizens Services Office, Room 4811 N.S., 2201 C St. NW, Washington, DC 20520; ☎ 202/647–5225 for interactive hot line; 301/946–4400 for computer bulletin board; FAX 202/647–3000 for interactive hot line; enclose a self-addressed, stamped, business-size envelope.

WEB SITES

Argentina phone book (www.guiatelefonica.com). **Argentina Secretary of Tourism** (www.sectur.gov.ar). **Buenos Aires Herald** (www.buenosairesherald. com). **Embassy of Argentina** (www.embassyofargentina-usa. org). **Tango** (www.abctango. com.ar).

WHEN TO GO

CLIMATE

Because of the great variety of latitudes, altitudes, and climatic zones in Argentina, you're likely to encounter many different climates during any given month. The most important thing to remember is the most obvious—**when it's summer in the Northern Hemisphere, it's winter in Argentina, and vice versa.** Winter in Argentina stretches from July to October and summer goes from December to March.

The sea moderates temperatures in most of Argentina's cities year-round. Winters can be chilly and rainy, though the average temperature is always above freezing and it hasn't snowed in Buenos Aires in more than 100 years. Summer is very tropical, hot, and muggy, which is most likely to send you indoors to the air-conditioning (if you can find it) at midday but makes for wonderful, warm nights.

If you can handle the heat (January–February temperatures usually range in the high 90s to low 100s [35°C–40°C]), Buenos Aires can be wonderful in summer, which peaks in January. At this time, the traditional vacation period, Argentines are crowding inland resorts and Atlantic beaches, but Buenos Aires has no traffic, and there is always a seat at shows and restaurants (though it can also feel a bit empty).

January is when most Porteños go on vacation—primarily to the Atlantic coast—which means that many businesses in Buenos Aires shut down and those that don't close have reduced hours (even most banks, except American Express). In February most banks and government offices open up again, but it's still school vacation, so many stores remain closed until early March.

If you have an aversion to large crowds, avoid visiting popular resort areas in January and February and in July, when they become overcrowded again due to school holidays.

Spring (October–early December) and fall (April–early June) are the best times to visit the city. It's usually warm enough (over 50°F) to travel with just a light jacket. Theater and sports seasons are just starting up or having their grand finales; and Porteños are excited about the summer vacation they've just had or the one they're about to take, so there's a heightened energy in the air.

► FORECASTS: **Weather Channel Connection** (☎ 900/932–8437), 95¢ per minute from a Touch-Tone phone.

The following are the average daily maximum and minimum temperatures for Buenos Aires.

Jan.	85F	29C	May	64F	18C	Sept.	64F	18C
	63	17		47	8		46	8
Feb.	83F	28C	June	57F	14C	Oct.	69F	21C
	63	17		41	5		50	10
Mar.	79F	26C	July	57F	14C	Nov.	76F	24C
	60	16		42	6		56	13
Apr.	72F	22C	Aug.	60F	16C	Dec.	82F	28C
	53	12		43	6		61	16

1 Destination: Buenos Aires

BARRIO CHIC

BUENOS AIRES, THE ninth-largest city in the world and the hub of the southern cone, is a sprawling megalopolis that rises from the Río de la Plata and stretches more than 200 sq km (75 sq mi) to the surrounding pampas, the fertile Argentine plains. It's the political, economic, and cultural capital of Argentina and the gateway to the rest of the country. Buenos Aires is bustling and alive with activity, from its vast museums and Parislike avenues to its late-night *asados* (barbecues) and tango performances.

In the Capital Federal, as this sprawling metropolis is known, 10 million people (⅓ the population of Argentina) live in the city's 47 *barrios* (neighborhoods), each with its own character, its own story to tell, and its own soccer team. Most residents of Buenos Aires have lived in the same barrio for their entire lives and feel much more of an affinity to their neighborhood than to the city as a whole.

Unlike most South American cities, where the architecture principally reveals a strong Spanish colonial influence, Buenos Aires has a mix of architectural styles. Block after block of tidy high-rise apartment buildings are interspersed with 19th-century houses. Neighborhoods such as Palermo, La Recoleta, and Belgrano feel more like Paris, with wide boulevards lined with palatial mansions, luxury high-rises, and spacious parks. Flowers are sold at colorful corner kiosks, the smell of freshly baked bread wafts out of well-stocked bakeries, terrace cafés can be found on every block, and pedestrians carry themselves with a fashionable reserve that is remarkably Parisian. In fact, Belgrano's vast neighborhood park is an exact replica of one in Paris. Its Church of the Immaculate Conception is modeled after Rome's Pantheon. Even the Vatican Embassy on Avenida Alvear is a copy of the Jacquemart-André Museum in Paris. Other neighborhoods, such as San Telmo and La Boca, have a distinctly working-class Italian feel. Many have compared the Plaza de Mayo, principally the Avenida de Mayo, to Budapest; and the Galerías Pacífico, a shopping mall in the center of the city, was built to look like Galleria Vittorio Emanuele in Milan.

Buenos Aires locals are referred to as *Porteños* because many of them originally arrived by boat from Europe and started out in the city's port area, La Boca. Porteños are known as thinkers—they enjoy philosophical discussions and psychoanalysis (as proven by the large number of psychoanalysts per capita—in fact, the most of any city in the world). The citizens seem perpetually confused about their national identity—South American or European?—and are often concerned about how outsiders perceive them. Many are also deeply image-conscious, reflected in the lengths to which Porteñas go to be beautiful.

Buenos Aires has no Eiffel Tower, no internationally renowned museums, no must-see sights that clearly identify it as a world-class city. Rather, it provides a series of small interactions that have intense Latin spirit—a flirtatious glance, a heartfelt chat, a juicy steak, a beautiful tango—which combine to create a vibrant and unforgettable urban experience.

PLEASURES AND PASTIMES

Dining
Dining in Buenos Aires is an art, a passion, and a pastime. Whether at home or in restaurants, meals are events. *Sobremesa* (chatting after the meal) is just as important as the meal itself, and people linger at a table long after a meal is over. The staple is beef, which is usually cooked on the *parrilla* (grill) or barbecue (*asado*). A typical meal consists of a steak accompanied by meat, french fries, salad, and red wine.

Lodging
Buenos Aires has a mix of hotels, inns, and apart-hotels (short-term rental apartments). Although the city isn't known for its world-class facilities, it does have a few noteworthy establishments, including the Alvear Palace Hotel and the Park Hyatt. Note that in summer (January and February, in particular), when most locals are on vacation and restaurants may be empty and stores closed, Buenos Aires hotels still charge high-season rates.

Shopping
During the 1970s external trade was prohibited, so Argentines had to go abroad to buy quality foreign goods. Once trade was permitted again in the early 1990s, it opened up a floodgate of higher quality merchandise. This, combined with a more stable currency, has led to vastly increased selection and variety. Now it's possible to purchase not only high-quality Argentine silver and leather goods but also European fashions and clothes from such national designers as Paula Cahen D'Avers. Open-air markets are the best places to buy souvenirs such as a gourd specially designed for drinking *mate* (a local tealike beverage) or items made of silver.

FODOR'S CHOICE

Dining

★ **Los Años Locos.** Come to this low-key spot along Río de la Plata for long lunches and late-night steak dinners. *$$$*

★ **Cabaña las Lilas.** Join presidents, movie stars, and Porteños for the best meat in the city. *$$$$*

★ **Melo.** In Barrio Norte, Melo serves up traditional fare in a friendly atmosphere. *$–$$*

Historic Sights

★ **Cementerio de La Recoleta.** This cemetery is a veritable who's who of Argentine history.

Lodging

★ **Alvear Palace Hotel.** Built in 1932, the Alvear is the city's most elegant hotel. *$$$$*

★ **Park Hyatt.** The luxurious Park Hyatt has large rooms, great amenities, and an outstanding staff. *$$$$*

Museums

★ **Calle Museo Caminito.** This pedestrians-only street has functioned as an open-air museum and art market since 1959.

★ **Museo de Arte Española Enrique Larreta.** Once the home of a Spanish governor, the beautiful building now houses a superb collection of Spanish colonial art.

GREAT ITINERARIES

If You Have 3 Days

If you have only three days in Buenos Aires, you'll have time to appreciate the city—but at breakneck speed. Plan to spend a half day in each of the following areas: Plaza de Mayo, El Centro, La Boca, San Telmo, Palermo, and La Recoleta. If you're in town on a weekend, visit La Recoleta on Saturday and San Telmo on Sunday. If you're in town in the middle of the week, try to stick to Palermo on Monday, since its attractions are open (whereas most museums are closed on Monday). Remember to schedule time for a siesta since, with only two nights in the city, you'll want to spend one night out at a club, bar, or performance and the other enjoying an evening of tango.

If You Have 5 Days

With five days you can enjoy all of the sights described in the three-day itinerary above. You'll also have more time to explore La Recoleta or San Telmo as well as Puerto Madero and Belgrano.

2 Exploring Buenos Aires

BUENOS AIRES IS ENORMOUS and sprawling. You're best off exploring one neighborhood at a time by foot and taking public transportation—bus or *subte* (subway). Streets are basically laid out in a grid, though a few streets transverse the grid at 45-degree angles; these are helpfully called *diagonal*. *Avenidas* are two-way streets (at most hours of the day), while *calles* are generally one way. Each city block is exactly 100 meters long, and addresses are based on the building's measured position on the street, not by street number (for instance, 180 Calle Florida is 100 meters, or one block, from 80 Calle Florida).

San Telmo

The appealing if a bit run-down neighborhood of San Telmo, halfway between midtown Buenos Aires and the south end of the city, is comparable to New York's Greenwich Village. Its cobblestone streets are rich with early 19th-century colonial architecture and mansions, once inhabited by upper-class Spaniards. Over the years the mansions were converted into multifamily housing for the immigrant families (particularly Italians) who began moving to this neighborhood during the late 19th century. For the past 20 years these old houses have been transformed into shops, art galleries, restaurants, and bars. The neighborhood is a cradle of Buenos Aires history and culture (including the tango) and folkloric traditions. Neighborhood highlights include the Sunday flea market, the antiques shops along Calle Defensa, and the tango bars that come to life nightly.

Numbers in the text correspond to numbers in the margin and on the San Telmo map.

A Good Walk

To reach San Telmo from anywhere in the city, take Line E to the Independencia stop; from here it's an eight-block walk down Calle Estados Unidos to Calle Defensa. **Plaza Dorrego** ①, at the corner of Calles Defensa and Humberto Primo, is the focal point of San Telmo and the home of the Sunday flea market. Marking the southern edge of San

Telmo are the gardens of the **Parque Lezama** ②; the Lezama home is now the **Museo Histórico Nacional** ③. Overlooking the park, visible above the trees lining Avenida Brasil, are the onion-shape domes of the **Iglesia Ortodoxa Rusa** ④. Continue north from the park along Calle Defensa, which is lined with shops and tenement apartment buildings. The street leads past many of the city's best art spaces, including the **Fundación del Rotary Club** ⑤ and the **Museo de Arte Moderno** ⑥. San Telmo's antiques shopping district begins at the corner of Calle Defensa and Avenida San Juan. Close to the corner of the Plaza Dorrego, on Calle Humberto Primo, stands a small chapel, **Nuestra Señora del Carmen** ⑦. The adjoining cloister, which later became a hospice and then a prison for women, is now the **Museo Penitenciario Antonio Balve** ⑧. A few relics of the colonial period are still found on Calle Carlos Calvo, just off Calle Defensa, including the **Pasaje Giuffra** ⑨ along with its neighbor, the **Pasaje de la Defensa** ⑩, and **La Casa de Esteban de Luca** ⑪. Continuing along Calle Defensa, take a right on on Calle Independencia to get to the famous **Viejo Almacén** ⑫.

TIMING AND PRECAUTIONS

Plan to go to San Telmo on a Sunday, when the market on Plaza Dorrego bustles with life and there are performers singing and dancing on every corner. A few hours will give you plenty of time to see the sights, but you could easily spend a full day exploring the side streets and shops. San Telmo is one of the city's seedier districts, and you should exercise caution when walking here—especially at night. Violent crime is rare, but unemployment in San Telmo and its neighboring barrios, combined with the knowledge that foreign tourists will always hit the area for at least one tango show, has led to increased instances of pickpocketing and muggings.

Sights to See

⑪ **La Casa de Esteban de Luca** (Esteban de Luca's House). This old home, now a typical Argentine restaurant, was declared a National Historic Monument in 1941. It belonged to Esteban de Luca, a distinguished poet and soldier who wrote Argentina's first national anthem. It's a great place to stop for a bite, taking in a bit of history with your Argentine wine. ⊠ *Defensa 1000,* ☎ *11/4361–4338.*

8

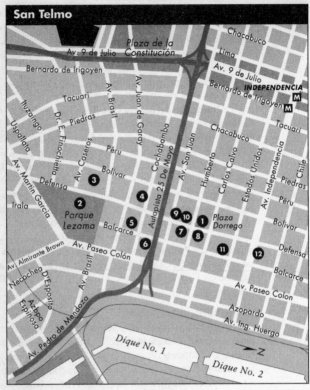

San Telmo

❺ Fundación del Rotary Club (Rotary Club Foundation). The Rotary Club Foundation, housed in a fine postcolonial house with an enclosed courtyard, puts on monthly shows by contemporary Argentine and international artists and hosts concerts. ✉ *Defensa 1344,* ☎ *11/4361–5485.* 🎟 *Free.* ⊙ *Weekdays after 4 (call for exact concert times), Sat. 8–8.*

❹ Iglesia Ortodoxa Rusa (Russian Orthodox Church). The church with its sky blue dome was hastily built in the late 1910s by the eclectic Danish architect Alejandro Cristophersen for the congregation of Russians who had settled in the city. The property, strangely, still belongs to Russia. ✉ *Av. Brasil 315.* ⊙ *Sat. 6 PM–8:30 PM, Sun. 10 AM–12:30 PM.*

❻ Museo de Arte Moderno (Modern Art Museum). This old cigarette factory with a classical brick facade has been transformed into the Museum of Modern Art. It holds temporary shows by local painters and sculptors and permanent exhibits of prominent international contemporary artists. It's often possible to meet the artists here—in lectures or just hanging out at the gallery—discussing their own works and those of others. ✉ *Av. San Juan 350,* ☎ *11/4361–1121.* 🎟 *Admission; free on Wed.* ⊙ *Tues.–Fri. 10–8, weekends and holidays 11–8.*

★ **❸ Museo Histórico Nacional** (National Historical Museum). The Lezama family home, an example of a stately but decaying old mansion, is now the National Historical Museum. The focus is on the official history of Argentina from the 16th century to the beginning of the 1900s. Most prominently displayed are memorabilia relating to General José de San Martín and his campaigns in 1810 during the War of Independence against Spain. The jewel of the museum is the collection of paintings by Cándido López, a forceful precursor of contemporary primitive painting. López, who lost an arm in the Paraguayan War of the 1870s, which Paraguay fought against Argentina and Brazil, learned to paint with his left hand and produced an exciting series of war scenes on a scale that would have captivated Cecil B. DeMille. ✉ *Defensa 1600,* ☎ *11/4307–1182.* 🎟 *Free.* ⊙ *Feb.–Dec., Tues.–Sun. noon–6.*

❽ Museo Penitenciario Antonio Balve (Antonio Balve Penitentiary Museum). This modest museum has mementos of early 20th-century prison life. Behind the museum's large courtyard is **Nuestra Señora del Carmen** (☞ *below*). Next door is an even larger church, the **Parroquia de San Pedro González Telmo** (San González Telmo Parish Church). ✉ *Humberto Primero 378.* 💵 *Admission.* ⊙ *Weekdays 10–noon and 2–5; Sun. noon–6.*

7 Nuestra Señora del Carmen. This chapel behind the Museo Penitenciario Antonio Balve's (☞ *above*) large courtyard dates from the Jesuit period. Next door is the **Parroquia de San Pedro González Telmo** (San González Telmo Parish Church), which was abandoned halfway through its construction by the Jesuits in 1767, when the order was expelled from Argentina, and was not completed until 1858. The cloisters and the domed chapel to the left, designed by Father Andrés Blanqui in 1738, are the only remnants of the original structure. ✉ *Humberto Primero 378.*

2 Parque Lezama (Lezama Park). Enormous magnolia, palm, cedar, and elm trees fill the sloping hillside, and winding paths lead down to the river. The land fell into the hands of an English family in the 1840s, who sold it to George Ridgely Horne, an American businessman, who in turn sold it in 1858 to Gregorio Lezama, an entrepreneur. Lezama decorated the gardens of his luxurious estate with life-size statues and enormous urns. At the end of the 19th century, his widow donated the property to the city, and it has since become a popular spot for family picnics on weekends. On Sunday an arts and crafts market takes place. ✉ *Brasil and Paseo Colón.* 💵 *Free.* ⊙ *Daily, dawn–dusk.*

10 Pasaje de la Defensa (Defense Alley). This alleyway gives you an idea of what Buenos Aires looked like 200 years ago. ✉ *Off Calle Defensa.*

9 Pasaje Giuffra (Giuffra Alley). A glimpse down this short alley running toward the river gives you a feel for the old city. ✉ *Off Calle Defensa.*

★ **1 Plaza Dorrego** (Dorrego Square). On weekdays this square with outdoor tables shaded by stately old trees provides a peaceful haven for chess-playing pensioners. On Sunday from 10 to 5 the plaza comes alive with the bustling **San Telmo Antiques Fair.** Often you'll find a young couple dancing frenzied tangos on one corner to the music of veteran tango musicians playing violins and *bandoneons* (the local version of the accordion). The fair provides a great opportunity to buy tango memorabilia, leather goods, high-quality silver, and a wide variety of Argentine knickknacks. The buildings surrounding the plaza provide a sampling of the architectural styles—Spanish colonial, French classical, and lots of ornately decorated masonry done by Italian craftsmen—that gained a significant presence in the city in the 19th and 20th centuries.

⑫ **Viejo Almacén.** This popular nightspot for tango (☞ Chapter 5) is another fine example of colonial architecture. The building dates from 1798, during which time it was a general store (Almacén de Campaña). After a stint as a hospital in the 1800s, the building was purchased by Paula Kravnic, the daughter of a Russian immigrant, who transformed it into a tango bar at the turn of the 20th century. The bar gained even greater popularity when it was purchased, in 1969, by Argentine tango sensation Eduardo Rivero. ⊠ *Av. Independencia.*

La Boca

The vibrant working-class neighborhood of La Boca is the southern neighbor of San Telmo. The first port of Buenos Aires, La Boca has seen many waves of immigrant populations pass through its borders. The most significant and lasting group were Italian immigrants from Genoa, who arrived between 1880 and 1930. Still known as the Little Italy of Argentina, La Boca is the perfect place to find an authentic and inexpensive pizza or an impromptu tango lesson in the street.

Numbers in the text correspond to numbers in the margin and on the La Boca map.

A Good Walk

Your entire experience in La Boca will probably center around the **Calle Museo Caminito** ⑬, an outdoor art market and museum right off Avenida Pedro de Mendoza. Once you reach the end of the Caminito, turn right on Calle Garibaldi. Four blocks down the street is the imposing

Estadio de Boca Juniors ⑭, home to one of the most popular soccer teams in Argentina. Take a right on Calle Brandsen and another right on Calle del Valle Iberlucea to get back to the entrance to the Caminito. To your left on Avenida Pedro de Mendoza is the **Museo de Bellas Artes de La Boca de Artistas Argentinos** ⑮, a noteworthy neighborhood museum.

TIMING AND PRECAUTIONS

You could easily spend an entire day in La Boca, meandering about and taking in the sights, but you really only need 1½–2 hours to see everything. It's best to stay in the area of the Caminito, which is well patrolled by local police, and not to stray too far, as the neighborhood borders other barrios that aren't very safe. There are few reasons for you to go to La Boca at night, and it would be safer not to do so. Note that La Boca is the land of the unleashed dog: Beware where you step, and certainly remember that while neighborhood dogs are accustomed to people, they may not react kindly to being petted.

Sights to See

★ ⑬ **Calle Museo Caminito** (Caminito Museum Street). The Caminito is a colorful pedestrians-only street that since 1959 has functioned as an open-air museum and art market. It's only about a block and a half long, but you can find numerous quality souvenirs, sculptures, and free open-air tango demonstrations. Walking along the Caminito, notice the distinctive, rather hastily constructed architecture, which is often painted in vibrant colors to cover shoddy materials. ⊠ *Av. Pedro de Mendoza and Calle Palos.* 🎟 *Free.* ☉ *Daily 10–6.*

⑭ **Estadio de Boca Juniors** (Boca Juniors Stadium). The Boca Juniors are one of Argentina's most popular soccer teams and, as such, are the proud owners of a very distinctive stadium. If you have the chance to visit the stadium on a game day, be prepared for crowds, pandemonium, and street parties—and never wear red and white, the colors of River Plate, the rival team! ⊠ *Brandsen 805.*

⑮ **Museo de Bellas Artes de La Boca de Artistas Argentinos** (La Boca Fine Arts Museum of Argentine Artists). This local fine arts museum is worth a visit, as it provides a good overview

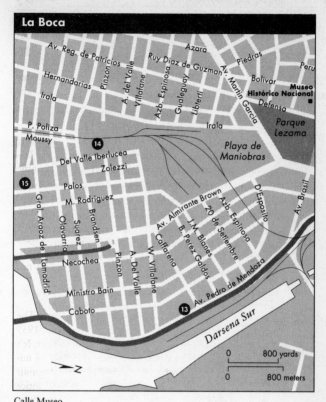

La Boca

Calle Museo
Caminito, **13**

Estadio
de Boca
Juniors, **14**

Museo de
Bellas Artes de
La Boca de
Artistas
Argentinos, **15**

of Argentine artistic history. It closes in summer for renovation and to set up new exhibits, so it's wise to call ahead
to see if it's open. ⊠ *Av. Pedro de Mendoza 1835,* ☎ *11/
4301–1080.* 🖃 *Free.* ◷ *Weekdays 8–6, weekends 10–5.*

Plaza de Mayo

In a well-known scene in the musical *Evita,* Eva Perón
stands on a picturesque balcony and waves to the Argentine masses assembled on a square below. She is supposed
to be here, at the Plaza de Mayo. The political and historical center of Buenos Aires, the square is home to the presidential palace and other governmental buildings. It has
survived wars, floods, and political upheaval; on every corner you see evidence of its history. Its attractions are principally architectural—the cathedral, where you may catch
site of visiting dignitaries (as well as Argentina's president)
at Sunday services, and some well-preserved remnants of
Spanish colonial architecture.

*Numbers in the text correspond to numbers in the margin
and on the Plaza de Mayo and Centro map.*

A Good Walk

Get your bearings at the **Plaza de Mayo** ⑯. At the eastern
end of the square, the Casa de Gobierno (Presidential Office Building), better known as the **Casa Rosada** ⑰, dominates the view toward the river. At the far western end of
Avenida de Mayo is the tall dome that's home to Argentina's parliament, the **Congreso** ⑱. All along Avenida
de Mayo, which was built in the manner of a Parisian
boulevard (although more often compared to avenues in
Budapest), are sidewalk cafés and interesting buildings.
Across Avenida Rivadavía, adding a conservative tone to
the plaza's profile, is the **Banco de la Nación Argentina** ⑲.
On the next block is the **Catedral Metropolitana** ⑳, which
hardly looks like a Latin-American church. Continue to the
plaza's west side to see the historic town council building,
the **Cabildo** ㉑. Leaving the plaza, walk one block on Di-
aganol Sur to reach **La Manzana de las Luces** ㉒ and the Colegio Nacional, the country's leading public school. Next to
the school is Buenos Aires's oldest church, the **Parroquia
de San Ignacio** ㉓. Continue east on Calle Alsina to the **Museo**

de la Ciudad ㉔, which has exhibits on the history of Buenos Aires. Across Calle Defensa is the **Basilica y Convento de San Francisco** ㉕, a colonial-era church, and the smaller Capilla San Roque, to its left. Another of the city's oldest churches, **Santo Domingo** ㉖, is two blocks south on Calle Defensa. From here, you can reach Puerto Madero (☞ *below*) by walking five blocks east along Belgrano and then continuing north along the riverfront. Alternatively, you can get to Puerto Madero by walking directly east on Calle Alsina or Calle Mitre from Plaza de Mayo.

TIMING AND PRECAUTIONS

This walk will probably take about two hours, though you could easily spend a full day exploring all the sights in the area. To be safe when taking a taxi in this area, avoid hailing one in front of a bank because people will think you've just taken out money and may rob your cab; instead, hail one in front of a local coffee shop, where you're much less likely to be a potential victim of a robbery. On weekends the streets are deserted, so pay close attention to your belongings, especially when walking alone.

Sights to See

⑲ **Banco de la Nación Argentina** (National Bank of Argentina). This imposing state bank was designed in 1940 in monumental Neoclassical style by architect Alejandro Bustillo, who designed most of the city's government buildings in the 1930s and 1940s. ✉ *Corner of Reconquista and Rivadavia.*

㉕ **Basilica y Convento de San Francisco** (Convent and Basilica of St. Francis). Originally built in 1754, the Bavarian Baroque facade was added in 1911, and the interior was lavishly refurbished after the church was looted and burned in 1955 in the turmoil just before Perón's government fell. Inside, an archive of 20,000 books remains. ✉ *Defensa and Alsina,* ☎ *11/4331–0625.* ▣ *Free.*

㉑ **Cabildo** (Town Council). The town council building is considered one of Argentina's national shrines. In May 1810 patriotic citizens gathered here to vote against Spanish rule. The original building dates from 1765 but has been the product of successive renovations, the latest of which was in 1948. Inside is a small museum, but the building alone is worth the trip. After visiting this monument, you can't

16

Plaza de Mayo and Centro

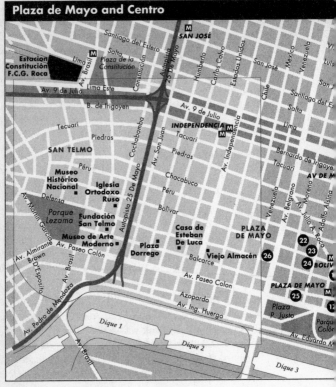

Santo
Domingo, **26**
Teatro Colón, **35**

help but notice how many places in the city are named Cabildo. ⊠ *Bolívar 65,* ☎ *11/4334–1782.* 🖂 *Free.* ☉ *Tues.–Fri. 12:30–7, Sun. 3–7; guided tours at 3 and 5.*

⑰ Casa Rosada (Pink House). The Casa de Gobierno (Government Palace), better known as the Casa Rosada, is the government headquarters (the president doesn't live here, though). The elite Grenadiers Regiment keeps close guard over the pale-pink house. The first-floor balcony on the building's northern wing is used by the country's leaders to address the enormous crowds that gather below. This is where Evita came to rally the workers and where Madonna sang her rendition of "Don't Cry for Me Argentina" (the window air-conditioning units were taken out for the movie). In back, on the basement level, the brick walls of the **Taylor Customs House**—which dates from the 1850s—have been partially uncovered after being buried for half a century, when the Plaza Colón was built. The site can be seen from the outside or as part of a visit to the adjoining **Museo de la Casa Rosada,** a museum containing presidential memorabilia. You may find it interesting that unlike a White House tour, the tour of the Casa Rosada Museum is relatively unsupervised, leading you to wonder just a little about security issues. ⊠ *Hipólito Yrigoyen 211,* ☎ *11/4343–3051 or 11/4374–9841 for guided tours.* 🖂 *Free; charge for guided tours.* ☉ *Mon.–Tues. and Thurs.–Fri. 10–6; Sun. 2–6; guided tours at 4.*

⑳ Catedral Metropolitana (Metropolitan Cathedral). The first building on this site was an adobe ranch house, which disappeared in 1593. Since then the land has been continually in use. But it wasn't until 1822 that the neoclassical facade of the Metropolitan Cathedral was begun (the building itself predates the facade by a century). The remains of General José de San Martín, known as the Argentine Liberator for his role in the War of Independence against Spain, are buried here in a marble mausoleum carved by the French sculptor Carrière Belleuse. The tomb is permanently guarded by soldiers of the Grenadier Regiment, a troop created and trained by San Martín in 1811. ⊠ *Rivadavía and San Martín,* ☎ *11/4331–2845.* 🖂 *Free.* ☉ *Guided tour weekdays 1:30, Sat. 10:30 and 11:15.*

⑱ Congreso. Built in 1906, the exterior was modeled after the U.S. Congress building. The building is surrounded by an attractive park, and is considered Kilometer 0 for every Argentine highway. It's not open to the public. ⊠ *Plaza del Congreso.*

㉒ La Manzana de las Luces (Block of Bright Lights). This block of buildings was constructed in the early 1800s on property that originally belonged to the Jesuits, who were expelled in 1767. Home to a succession of schools, it's famous as the breeding ground for Argentina's *intelligentsía* and it houses Argentina's most famous school. The bulky neoclassical building on the site, where the San Ignacio school once stood, is now home to the **Colegio Nacional,** the country's leading public high school. You can take a guided tour of La Manzana de las Luces and the surrounding area; though infrequent and conducted in Spanish, these tours are worthwhile (call to verify the times listed below, as tour times change frequently). Going on a tour is your only chance to view the cavernous, historic tunnels that run under La Manzana. The tours follow various routes: Circuit B brings you to the tunnels and nearby churches; Circuit C takes you to the tunnels and the old State Representatives room; Circuit D takes you through the Colegio Nacional; and Circuit E takes you to the tunnels and past historic local homes. ⊠ *Perú 272,* ☎ *11/4342–6973.* ✆ *Admission.* ☉ *Guided tours on weekends between 3 and 6:30.*

㉔ Museo de la Ciudad (Municipal Museum). This museum houses temporary exhibits both whimsical and probing about many aspects of domestic and public life in Buenos Aires in times past. On the ground floor, for instance, is the **Farmacia La Estrella** (Star Pharmacy), a quaint survivor from the 19th century. ⊠ *Calle Alsina 412,* ☎ *11/4331–9855 or 11/4343–2123.* ✆ *Admission.* ☉ *Weekdays 11–7, Sun. 3–7.*

㉓ Parroquia de San Ignacio (St. Ignatius Church). Started in 1713, this church is the only one from that era to have a Baroque facade. Behind the church, a neoclassical facade dating from 1863 hides the old colonial building that headquartered the administrators of the Jesuits' vast land holdings in northeastern Argentina and Paraguay. In 1780 the city's first Facultad de Medicina (Medical School) was established here, and in the early 19th century was home to the Universidad de Buenos Aires (University of Buenos Aires). The tunnels underneath the building, which criss-crossed the colonial town and were used either by the military or by smugglers, depending on which version you believe, can still be visited by guided tour (☞ La Manzana de las Luces, *above*). ⊠ *Bolívar 225,* ☎ *11/4331–2458.* ✉ *Free.* ☯ *Tours on weekends at 3:30 and 5.*

★ ⑯ **Plaza de Mayo** (May Square). This two-block-long square has been the stage for many important events, including the uprising against Spain on May 25, 1810, in memory of which the square was given its name. The present layout dates from 1912, when the obelisk known as the **Piramide de Mayo** was placed in the center; it was erected in 1811 to celebrate the first anniversary of the Revolution of May. A bronze equestrian statue of General Manuel Belgrano, cast in 1873, stands at the east end of the plaza. The tradition of staging celebrations and protests in this central plaza continues to this day. It's here that the Madres de la Plaza de Mayo (Mothers of Plaza de Mayo), the mothers of young *desaparecidos,* young people who "disappeared" during the military government's reign from 1976 to 1983, still hold their Thursday-afternoon marches, which attracted international attention during the late 1970s.

㉖ **Santo Domingo.** Built in the 1750s, this convent is dedicated to Our Lady of the Rosary. On display in the chapel are four banners captured in 1806 from fleeing British troops—after their unsuccessful attempt to invade the then-Spanish colony—and two flags taken from the Spanish armies during the War of Independence. On one of the bell towers, bullet craters—testimony to the battle with British soldiers—are reminders of the conflict. The remains of General Manuel Belgrano, a hero of the War of Independence, rest in the courtyard's central mausoleum, guarded by marble angels. ⊠ *Defensa 422,* ☎ *11/4331–1668.* ✉ *Free.*

El Centro

Your first glimpse of El Centro will most likely be en route from the airport. But be sure to return: Walking around the city center, dominated by a giant obelisk and the never-sleeping Avenida Corrientes, gives you a good feel for cosmopolitan Buenos Aires and its passionate Latin spirit. From the packed pedestrians-only Calle Florida and Calle Lavalle to the urban calm of Plaza San Martín, this is the social and business center of Argentina.

A Good Walk

El Centro can be reached by subte; in fact, every subway line goes through it. The most logical stop for this walk is called Estación 9 de Julio (alternately known as Estación Carlos Pelligrini), which puts you right at the obelisk as you exit the subway. The area is also accessible from Estación Plaza San Martín and Estación Lavalle.

Start your walk on **Plaza San Martín** ㉗. On one side of the park is the **Palacio San Martín** ㉘ and on another, the **Círculo Militar** ㉙. Across Calle Marcelo T. de Alvear from the Círculo, behind the sixth-floor windows of the corner apartment at No. 994 Calle Maipú, are the rooms where Jorge Luis Borges lived and wrote many of his short stories and poems. Also right here are the **Edificio Kavanagh** ㉚ and the landmark **Marriott Plaza Hotel** ㉛. The **Galería Ruth Benzacar** ㉜, with good exhibits of contemporary art, forms the entrance to Calle Florida, down a set of stairs. Take this crowded pedestrians-only shopping street south to get to one of Buenos Aires's nicest shopping centers, the **Galerías Pacífico** ㉝. Continue along Calle Florida until you reach Avenida Corrientes, the "street that never sleeps"; it's lined with theaters and cinemas and bustles with activity day and night. Turn right (west) and walk toward the giant **Obelisco** ㉞. The **Teatro Colón** ㉟ is two blocks north of the obelisk on vast Avenida 9 de Julio.

TIMING AND PRECAUTIONS

Set aside a full day to explore El Centro. It's an easy area to navigate on foot, though summer heat and crowds may leave you begging for air-conditioning. On weekdays it's packed, on Saturday it's relatively calm, and by Sunday it's nearly deserted. Many stores and most restaurants have limited hours on weekends. In January most businesses (including banks) in El Centro close, though some may have extremely limited hours. You'll notice as you meander along Calle Lavalle that, although it is a center of shopping and commerce, it's also home to many of the adult entertainment establishments in Buenos Aires. Take proper precautions when visiting the area at night.

Sights to See

㉙ Círculo Militar (Military Circle). A monument to the nobler historic pursuits of the Argentine armed forces, the Officers' Club was built by French architect Louis Sortais in 1902 in the heavily ornamental French style of the period. The **Museo Nacional de Armas** (National Arms Museum), in the basement, is packed with military memorabilia. ✉ *Av. Santa Fe 750,* ☎ *11/4311–1071.* ⌂ *Free.* ☉ *Mar.–Dec., Tues.–Fri. 2–7, Sat. 11–5, Sun. 1–6.*

㉚ Edificio Kavanagh (Kavanagh Building). The soaring Kavanagh apartment building was constructed in the 1930s in the then-popular Rationalist style by a displaced New Yorker. It's still one of the nicest-looking apartment buildings in the city. ✉ *On San Martín, a few doors down from Plaza San Martín.*

㉜ Galería Ruth Benzacar (Ruth Benzacar Gallery). This well-designed gallery has monthly shows of significant modern Argentine artists. If you want a stimulating overview of contemporary Argentine art, ask to see the vast collection of paintings in the basement. ✉ *Florida 1000,* ☎ *11/4313–8480.* ⌂ *Free.* ☉ *Mon–Sat. 9:30–8.*

㉝ Galerías Pacífico (Pacífico Shopping Center). The former headquarters of the Buenos Aires–Pacific Railway, the building was designed during Buenos Aires's turn-of-the-20th-century golden age as a copy of Milan's Gallerie Vittorio Emanuele. In 1992 it was turned into a glossy, multilevel American-style shopping mall. In an earlier renovation a large skylighted dome was added, and five leading Argentine artists were commissioned to paint murals (☞ Chapter 7). ✉ *Florida 753.*

NEED A BREAK?	On the second floor of the **Galerías Pacífico** (✉ Florida 753), above the ground-floor commotion, is a quiet oasis with comfortable couches and chairs, serving good coffee and champagne. It's right next to the information counter, where you can pick up brochures and maps.

㉛ Marriott Plaza Hotel. In 1908 local financier Ernesto Tornquist commissioned German architect Alfred Zucker to build
the Plaza Hotel, a building that—like its namesake in New
York City—still maintains its glow. ⊠ *Plaza San Martín.*

㉞ Obelisco (Obelisk). This enormous 221½-ft-tall obelisk is
one of the city's most prominent landmarks; it was built
in 1936 as part of a major public-works program. If you're
in Buenos Aires during an election or a major soccer match,
you'll witness crowds of Porteños surrounding the obelisk,
voicing their opinions about the day's events. ⊠ *Av. 9 de
Julio and Corrientes.*

㉘ Palacio San Martín (San Martín Palace). Once the residence of the Anchorena family, the palace has been the Min-
istry of Foreign Affairs since 1936. The ornate building,
designed in 1909 by Alejandro Cristophersen in grandiose
French neoclassical style, is an example of the turn-of-the-
20th-century opulence of Buenos Aires. It's not open to the
public. ⊠ *Arenales 800.*

OFF THE
BEATEN
PATH

**MUSEO DE ARTE HISPANOAMERICANO ISAAC FERNÁNDEZ
BLANCO** – Built as the residence of the architect Martín Noel
in the late 18th century in an eclectic post–Spanish colonial
style, it's now home to the Isaac Fernández Blanco His-
panic-American Art Museum. The extensive collection of
colonial silver, wood carvings, and paintings gives you a
sense of the wealth and the quality of craftsmanship in colonial South America. The overgrown, almost junglelike garden provides an awesome background for the outdoor
theatrical performances mounted here during the summer.
⊠ *Suipacha 1422,* ☎ *11/4327–0228.* 🎟 *Admission.*
🕑 *Feb.–Dec., Tues.–Sun. 2–8.*

㉗ Plaza San Martín (San Martín Square). Once a field in a
muddy suburb at the northern end of the city next to the
steep riverbank, Plaza San Martín gradually evolved into
its present state. At one time populated by vagrants and
marginal members of the rough-and-tumble colonial society, the area around the square was transformed in the late
1800s into the site of some of the most sumptuous town
houses in Buenos Aires. The imposing bronze equestrian
monument to General José de San Martín, created in 1862

by French artist Louis Daumas, dominates the park. French landscape architect Charles Thays designed the plaza in the 19th century, using a mix of traditional local and exotic imported trees. To get a feel for real life in Buenos Aires, plan a visit to Plaza San Martín during a weekday lunch hour and relax in the crowded park while you watch business deals being hashed out and young lovers sneaking a kiss.

NEED A BREAK?   Wouldn't now be perfect time for a great glass of Argentine wine in a cool, hidden grotto? Then head to **Tancat** (✉ Paraguay 645, ☎ 11/4312–5442), a dark, friendly establishment where you'll most likely end up sitting at the bar as there's only one table. The menu consists of whatever the chef decides to cook that day, but the food is always good.

★ ㉟   **Teatro Colón** (Colón Theater). This opera house opened in 1908 and has hosted the likes of Maria Callas, Arturo Toscanini, Igor Stravinsky, Enrico Caruso, and Luciano Pavarotti. Argentines proudly claim that the theater has the best acoustics in the world, and few would argue. The Italianate building with French decoration is the result of a joint effort by several successive turn-of-the-20th-century architects. The seven-tier theater has a central chandelier with a sprawling diameter of 21 ft. Yet because there are only 2,500 seats, many of which are held by season-ticket holders, the lines stretch around the block when an international celebrity is starring. A fascinating guided tour of the theater and museum provides a glimpse at the building's inner workshops, 45 ft below the street. The international season runs from April to November. ✉ *Toscanini 1180,* ☎ *11/4382–6632.* ⌑ *Admission.* ⊙ *Jan.–Mar., tours hourly weekdays 10–5; fewer tours in winter.*

Puerto Madero

The revived old port has witnessed the proliferation of offices and fine restaurants in the past few years, making it *the* place to enjoy a coffee or dinner and a walk along the riverfront boardwalk. The port was originally constructed in 1890 as the European gateway to Argentina but spent most of the 20th century abandoned due to the creation of a new port (Puerto Nuevo). In August 1998 Puerto Madero was honored as the 47th area to be designated a barrio of Buenos Aires, a tribute to its significant transformation.

Numbers in the text correspond to numbers in the margin and on the Puerto Madero map.

A Good Walk

Start off from the Leandro Alem subte station and walk down Avenida Corrientes toward the river. As you go, notice the change in architecture, from Spanish colonial buildings to modern glass high-rises and refurbished port buildings. Continue along Avenida Corrientes, across Calle Bouchard and past Luna Park (☞ Chapter 6), where many sporting events and concerts are held. Pass Avenida Eduardo Madero, and you are in Puerto Madero. (Note that Avenida Eduardo Madero and Avenida Ing. Huergo are the same street but that the name changes as you continue along the dock.) Walk one block more to get to the main drag of Puerto Madero: Avenida Alicia M. de Justo. Docked here is the **Buque Museo Fragata A.R.A. *Presidente Sarmiento*** ㊱, an impressive Argentine battleship that is now a museum (when it's not in use). At the end of the dock is Cine 8 (☞ Chapter 5), one of Buenos Aires's best cinemas. Take a break here with an Argentine or Hollywood film.

TIMING AND PRECAUTIONS

You could easily spend half a day just walking Puerto Madero's 15-block boardwalk. In the morning the dock is a nice place to sit outside and enjoy an espresso, during the day the port fills with the commotion of business transpiring, and in the evening it attracts a fashionable crowd that comes to dine in the many restaurants. Though Puerto Madero is well patrolled by both private security and Buenos Aires police, there are pickpockets, so you should keep an eye on your wallet both on the dock and in restaurants.

Sights to See

㊱ **Buque Museo Fragata A.R.A. *Presidente Sarmiento*** (*President Sarmiento* Ship Museum). A classic warship, the *Presidente Sarmiento* was constructed in 1898 and has completed 39 around-the-world voyages. When not being used for military training, it's docked and open to the public as a museum. ⊠ *Dique 3, Puerto Madero,* ☎ *11/4334–9386.* 🎫 *Admission.* ⊙ *Weekdays 9–8, weekends 9 AM–10 PM.*

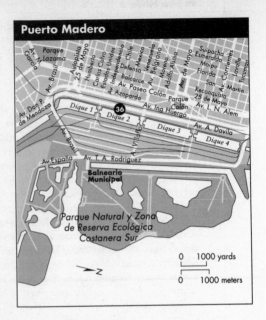

Puerto Madero

OFF THE
BEATEN
PATH

RESERVA ECOLÓJICA – If you find yourself feeling out of touch with nature, head to the Ecological Reserve, just a short taxi ride from Puerto Madero. A perfect spot for bike rides and nature walks, the reserve is said to be home to more than 500 species of birds. A guided tour of the reserve called "Walking under the Full Moon" (voluntary charge) is given at 8 PM daily. The reserve is in a prime location, and many real-estate developers have their eyes on it as a site for luxury office buildings, so most Porteños don't expect the park to be here much longer. ✉ *Av. Tristán Achával Rodríguez 1550,* ☎ *11/4315–1320.* 💲 *Donation requested.* ⊘ *Apr.–Dec., daily 8–6; Jan.–Mar., daily, 8–sunset.*

La Recoleta

La Recoleta, an elegant residential and shopping district northwest of downtown, is packed with boutiques, cafés, handsome old apartment buildings, plazas, museums, and cultural centers. Once a neighborhood where nobody wanted to live, today La Recoleta is one of Buenos Aires's most sought-after districts, surpassed in trendiness only recently by Puerto Madero (☞ *above*). About 25 years ago a few brave entrepreneurs decided to take advantage of its low rents, opening some of the city's best restaurants. Upscale, European-style boutiques followed, and then members of Argentina's high society began moving here as well. Part of La Recoleta is now closed to traffic, and street-side cafés dot the area. Here people-watching is a highly developed art form, practiced predominantly by the perennially tanned and trim.

Numbers in the text correspond to numbers in the margin and on the La Recoleta map.

A Good Walk

No subte route directly serves La Recoleta. The closest stop is Estación Pueyrredón, an eight-block walk south (plans, however, are in the works for a new subway line which is supposed to service the area by the year 2001).

Begin your walk on **Plazoleta Carlos Pelligrini** ㊲. On one side is the **Alzaga Unzué** ㊳. Follow Avenida Alvear, Buenos Aires's most elegant avenue, lined with some of the best in French-style architecture and boutiques and the beautiful **Alvear Palace Hotel** ㊴. Continue along Avenida Alvear to get to the **Cementerio de La Recoleta** ㊵, the final resting place for some of Argentina's most distinguished citizens. Bordering the cemetery is the **Basílica del Pilar** ㊶. Just down the block from the basilica is the **Centro Cultural La Recoleta** ㊷, where art shows and performances are held. Below the cultural center is the Design Center (☞ Chapter 7), a mall filled entirely with home-furnishings stores. To your right, at the bottom of the hill, is the yellow **Palais de Glace–Salas Nacionales de Cultura** ㊸, which hosts all kinds of temporary exhibits. From here walk west along Avenida del Libertador, past Plaza Francia and **Plaza Mitre** ㊹ to get to the **Museo Nacional de Bellas Artes** ㊺, the city's major art museum, the **Biblioteca Nacional** ㊻, a modern library, and the **Museo Nacional de Arte Decorativo** ㊼, a decorative arts museum in an impressive neoclassical building.

TIMING AND PRECAUTIONS

Count on at least half a day to explore La Recoleta, though you could easily spend a morning or afternoon in the cemetery or art museum alone. In general, this is one of the city's safest areas and can be visited day and night.

Sights to See

㊲ Alvear Palace Hotel. The city's most traditional, old-world hotel opened its doors in 1932. It remains a principal gathering place for the Porteño elite. The elegant lobby is a great spot to stop for tea or a drink (☞ Chapter 4). ⊠ *Av. Alvear 1891,* ☎ *11/4808–2100 or 11/4804–7777.*

㊳ Alzaga Unzué. This French Renaissance–style house built in the late 19th century was saved from demolition by a group of local conservationists in the Perón era. Now a part of the Park Hyatt Hotel (☞ Chapter 4), the tower of the hotel rises from what was once the garden, and the old house is now called La Mansion. ⊠ *Posadas 1086.*

㊶ Basílica del Pilar (Basilica of the Pillar). In 1732 Franciscan monks built this church and cloister complex, which are fine examples of early colonial Baroque. The principal altar is made of engraved silver from Peru. Today the church is a popular place for weddings, and you can sometimes see the elegantly dressed guests mingling with the craftspeople who hold a weekend fair on the slopes of the adjoining park. ⊠ *Junin 1898,* ☎ *11/4803–6793.* ⊠ *Free.* ⊙ *Weekdays 7:30–1 and 4–8:30, weekends 1–6.*

㊻ Biblioteca Nacional (National Library). It took three decades to build the National Library, which was finally inaugurated in 1991. The eccentric modern building was the result of a design competition won by Argentine architects Clorindo Testa and Francisco Bullrich. ⊠ *Aguero 2502,* ☎ *11/4806–6155.* ⊠ *Free.* ⊙ *Mon.–Sat. 10–7.*

★ ㊵ Cementerio de La Recoleta (La Recoleta Cemetery). As you enter the tall, ominous gates of the vast, 13½-acre La Recoleta Cemetery, you can feel history around you. You may sense the wealth as well, since this is the costliest bit of land in all of Argentina, and it contains the elaborate mausoleums of presidents, political leaders, soldiers, authors, and other heroes of Argentina's history. The cemetery also functions as a mini-tour of art, sculpture, and architecture. Mausoleums were built to resemble chapels, Greek temples, pyramids, and scaled-down versions of family homes. In

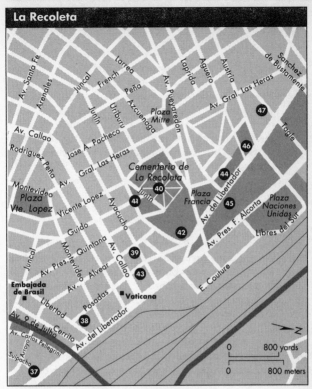

La Recoleta

Alvear Palace Hotel, **39**

Alzaga Unzué, **38**

Basílica del Pilar, **41**

Biblioteca Nacional, **46**

Cementario de La Recoleta, **40**

Centro Cultural La Recoleta, **42**

Museo Nacional de Arte Decorativo, **47**

Museo Nacional de Bellas Artes, **45**

Palais de Glaces—Salas Nacionales de Cultura, **43**

Plaza Mitre, **44**

Plazoleta Carlos Pelligrini, **37**

some you need to go inside to see what's special about them; for a small tip it's often possible to get a caretaker to open one of the multifloor mausoleums for you so that you look inside. The embalmed body of Eva Duarte de Perón rests here in the Duarte family tomb. To find Evita, from the entrance walk straight to the first major crossway and turn left; walk straight until a mausoleum stands in your way; walk around it on the right and then turn right; continue three rows down and turn left (or, just follow the sea of tourists who pay tribute to her at her tomb). Look, too, for the flowers placed on the tomb and the epitaph in Spanish that reads "Don't Cry for Me." Also worth looking for is the handsome statue of Luis Angel Firpo, the world heavyweight boxing champion known as the Bull of the Pampas. There's no map of the cemetery, so be prepared to walk in circles. ⊠ *Entrance on Junin.* ☉ *Daily 10–5.*

㊷ Centro Cultural La Recoleta (La Recoleta Cultural Center). On weekends this cultural center attracts thousands of visitors to its exhibits, concerts, and performances. It's also a resource for other arts events happening around the city. ⊠ *Junin 1930,* ☎ *11/4803–1041.* ▣ *Free.* ☉ *Tues.–Sat. after 2 (call for specific hrs), all day Sun.*

OFF THE BEATEN PATH

EMBAJADA DE BRASIL – This building—now the Brazilian Embassy—has a stately neoclassical facade. But inside is an even better treasure: a series of murals by Spanish artist José Luis Sert covers the walls and ceilings. Unfortunately, it's not open to the public. ⊠ *Arroyo 1142.*

EMBAJADA DE FRANCIA – Now the French Embassy, this building was once the home of the Ortiz Basualdo family. The house was designed in the early 20th century by French architect Phillipe Pater; the building is of such monumental importance that the city decided to loop the continuation of Avenida 9 de Julio around the back of it rather than razing the structure. Unfortunately, it's not open to the public. ⊠ *Cerrito 1339.*

★ ㊼ Museo Nacional de Arte Decorativo (National Museum of Decorative Art). This museum is in a magnificent French Classical landmark building (it's worth the price of admission just to enter this breathtaking structure). It houses a fascinating collection of furnishings and home decor; most was donated by Argentina's leading families. Also here is the **Museo de Arte Oriental** (Museum of Eastern Art), which has art and articles from places such as India and the Middle East. The museum café is great for a snack. ⊠ *Av. del Libertador 1902,* ☎ *11/4801–8248.* 🎟 *Admission.* ⊘ *Weekdays 2–8, weekends 11–7.*

🆔 **Museo Nacional de Bellas Artes** (National Museum of Fine Arts). Buenos Aires's only major art museum is housed in a building that was once the city's waterworks. The museum's collection includes several major Impressionist paintings and an overview of 19th- and 20th-century Argentine art. The highlight is a room dedicated to Paraguayan War scenes painted by a soldier, Cándido López, whose work is also in the National Historical Museum (☞ San Telmo, *above*). The new wing has a selection of contemporary Argentine art and temporary exhibits. ⊠ *Av. del Libertador 1473,* ☎ *11/4803–0802 for a tour.* 🎟 *Free.* ⊘ *Tues.–Sun. 12:30–7:30.*

🆔 **Palais de Glace–Salas Nacionales de Cultura** (Mirror Palace–National Cultural Exhibition Halls). Always worth checking out are the changing exhibitions, ranging from fine art to ponchos to national foods. The banner outside will tell you what's going on. ⊠ *Posadas 1725,* ☎ *11/4805–4354.* 🎟 *Admission.* ⊘ *Weekdays 1–8, weekends 3–8.*

🆔 **Plaza Mitre.** A large equestrian statue of General Bartolomé Mitre, the military hero and former president, dominates this square. The site, which was once at the edge of the river, provides a perspective on the surrounding parks. ⊠ *Avenida del Libertador between Calle Luis Agote and Calle Aguero.*

🆔 **Plazoleta Carlos Pellegrini** (Carlos Pellegrini Square). This square is surrounded by a cluster of mansions, which were once residences of the country's large landowning families and are now apartment buildings.

Palermo

Palermo, a district of parks and lakes surrounded by quiet streets and elegant mansions, offers a peaceful escape from the rush of downtown Buenos Aires. Families flock to the parks on weekends to picnic, suntan, bicycle, rollerblade, and jog. Palermo is also home to the polo field and the horse racetrack and is thus the center of horse culture in Buenos Aires. One of the city's largest barrios, Palermo has many distinct sub-neighborhoods: *Palermo Viejo* has classic Spanish-style architecture, *Las Cañitas* is a trendy place to go out at night, and *Palermo Chico* is an elegant residential area. Some of the most expensive real estate in Argentina is found along Avenida del Libertador, which cuts Palermo down the middle. But don't let Palermo's daytime tranquillity fool you: At night it gives way to some of the city's best nightlife, as neighborhood bars and discos rock to Latin beats.

Numbers in the text correspond to numbers in the margin and on the Palermo map.

A Good Walk

The Estación Plaza Italia, on Line D, takes you to the zoo and the botanical gardens in Palermo. Some of city's biggest parks are found in this neighborhood around the **Plaza Italia** ㊽, at the intersection of Avenida Sarmiento, Calle Santa Fe, and Calle Las Heras: the **Jardín Botánico** ㊾; the **Jardín Zoológico** ㊿; and the **Sociedad Rural Argentina** ㉛, the city's fairgrounds. Palermo's largest park, the **Parque Tres de Febrero** ㉜, is farther down Avenida Sarmiento. Essentially a part of the park, though technically freestanding, the **Paseo del Rosedal** ㉝ is abloom, in season, with all kinds of roses. Deeper into the park is the **Jardín Japonés** ㉞, a lovely Japanese garden, and the **Planetario Galileo Galilei** ㉟, the planetarium.

TIMING AND PRECAUTIONS

An even-paced ramble through Palermo should take no more than two hours, though you could easily spend an entire afternoon at the zoo, the Japanese Garden, and the Botanical Garden. If you're up for shopping, visit Alto Palermo (☞ Chapter 7), one of the city's nicer shopping centers (at the Bulnes stop on the D line), and the neighboring small boutiques along Avenida Santa Fe.

Sights to See

㊾ **Jardín Botánico** (Botanical Garden). The Botanical Garden is a welcome, unexpected oasis in the city. Enclosed by large wrought-iron gates, it's hard to imagine the beauty inside

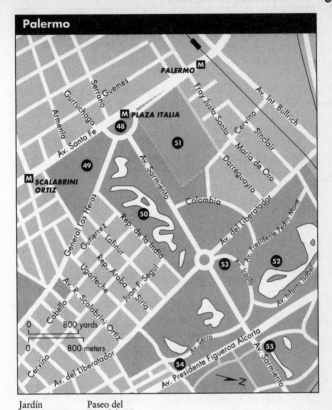

Palermo

until you enter. Modeled after an 18th-century French garden, the long, winding paths and hidden statues conjure up images of the gardens at Versailles. ⊠ *Av. Santa Fe 3817,* ☎ *11/4831–2951.* 🎫 *Free.* ☉ *Dawn–dusk.*

NEED A BREAK? Near the Botanical Garden and steps away from the Palermo Polo field is **La Cátedra** (⊠ at Cerviño and Sinclair, ☎ 11/4777–4601), a perfect spot for lunch or a drink. In good weather you can eat outdoors.

★ ❺❹ **Jardín Japonés** (Japanese Garden). This unexpected haven, run by the Japanese Cultural Society, is a fine Japanese garden. It has streams, bridges, and fishponds (you can buy food to feed the already well-fed fish). The garden is particularly beautiful at sunset. ⊠ *Avs. Casares and Adolfo Berro,* ☎ *11/4804–4922.* 🎫 *Admission.* ☉ *Dawn–dusk.*

✋ ❺⓪ **Jardín Zoológico** (Zoological Garden). The Buenos Aires zoo, where you'll find indigenous monkeys, birds, and many other animals, is a popular weekend destination for families. The animals aren't always kept in cages according to species type, so be prepared to see some interesting and unexpected cage mates. At the entrance to the zoo you can get a horse-drawn carriage to take you through the zoo and the Botanical Garden. ⊠ *República de la India 2900,* ☎ *11/4806–7412.* 🎫 *Admission.*

✋ ❺❷ **Parque Tres de Febrero** (February Third Park). Palermo's main park, just north of Calle Sarmiento, has 1,000 acres of woods, lakes, and walking trails. Paddle boats can be rented for use on the small lakes, and joggers, bikers, and rollerbladers all compete for the right of way on the miles of paved lanes. It's packed on weekends, with cars parked on the grass and soccer balls flying everywhere. Drinks and snacks are available at one of the park's cafés as well as along Avenida del Libertador.

NEED A BREAK? Have a snack or coffee in the café of the **Museo Renault** (⊠ Av. Figueroa Alcorta 3399, ☎ 11/4802–9626), about a 10-minute walk from the Parque Tres de Febrero.

★ ❺❸ **Paseo del Rosedal** (Rose Garden). The Rose Garden is a picturesque park full of fountains, statues of literati, and roses. On a Saturday in spring you're practically guaranteed to see a wedding here. ✉ *Av. del Libertador and Paseo de la Infanta.*

(55) **Planetario Galileo Galilei** (Galileo Galilei Planetarium). This planetarium on the western side of the Parque Tres de Febrero presents weekend-afternoon astronomy shows. ✉ *Sarmiento and Belisario Roldán,* ☎ *11/4771–6629.*

(48) **Plaza Italia.** This busy square at the intersection of Calle Santa Fe, Calle Las Heras, and Calle Sarmiento is a landmark in the area and a good place to meet. On weekends there's a crafts fair. ✉ *Santa Fe and Thames.*

(51) **Sociedad Rural Argentina** (Rural Society of Argentina). Exhibitions relating to agriculture and cattle raising are often held at the fairgrounds here. The biggest is the annual monthlong (usually in August) **Exposición Rural** (Rural Exposition), where you can see livestock such as cows and horses, gaucho shows, and expert horse performances. ✉ *Av. Las Heras 4051,* ☎ *11/4774–1072.*

Belgrano

Primarily a residential area, the fashionable, quiet district of Belgrano is home to beautiful mansions, luxury high-rises, and well-kept cobblestone streets leading off bustling Avenida Cabildo.

Numbers in the text correspond to numbers in the margin and on the Belgrano map.

A Good Walk

To reach Belgrano, take Line D to the last stop (Estación Virrey del Piño, though by the beginning of 2000 the last stop was slated to be Juramento, which is closer).

Head first to the **Museo de Arte Española Enrique Larreta** (56) for a taste of Spanish colonial art. Then cross the street to the **Museo Histórico Sarmiento** (57), which is essentially a shrine to independence from Spain. From here walk across the small **Plaza Manuel Belgrano** (58) to reach the **Parroquia de Nuestra Señora de la Inmaculada Concepción** (59). After visiting the church, take a break at one of the many cafés nearby. Two blocks along Calle Juramento from the church, across busy Avenida Cabildo, is the **Mercado** ⑥⓪, an open-air food market; it's worth the seemingly treacherous avenue crossing to experience this traditional market. Go in the other direction on Calle Juramento and take a right on Calle Tres de Febrero, a fancy residential street, to get to the **Museo Nacional del Hombre** ⑥①, an anthropology museum.

TIMING AND PRECAUTIONS

This walk can be done in two to three hours, though you could easily spend more time wandering around this beautiful barrio. If you want to see all the museums, it's best to visit in the afternoon, when they're all open. The atmospheric cafés around the church are open 24 hours. Belgrano is one of the safest districts in Buenos Aires: It's patrolled around the clock by private security and city police, and there's rarely any crime, except for the occasional purse snatching.

Sights to See

⑥⓪ **Mercado** (Market). This open-air local market is a treasure trove of everything you'd expect to find—cheese, fresh vegetables, and local meat—as well as a few surprises. Vendors bring their wares straight from local farms, and bartering and bargaining is common. ✉ *Juramento and Ciudad de la Paz.* ⊙ *Daily 5 PM–11 PM.*

★ ⑤⑥ **Museo de Arte Española Enrique Larreta** (Enrique Larreta Museum of Spanish Art). Once the beautiful home and gardens of a Spanish governor, the building now houses one of the best collections of Spanish colonial art in Argentina. ✉ *Juramento 2291,* ☎ *11/4783-2640.* ✆ *Admission; Tues. free.* ⊙ *Mon.–Tues. and Fri. 2–7:45, weekends 3–7:45.*

⑤⑦ **Museo Histórico Sarmiento** (Sarmiento Historical Museum). This charming colonial-style museum gives you yet another opportunity to learn about the history of Argentina through all kinds of art and artifacts. *Cuba 2079,* ☎ *11/4783-7555.* ✆ *Admission.* ⊙ *Tues.–Fri. and Sun. 3–8. Guided tours are available in Spanish at 4 PM Sun.*

⑥① **Museo Nacional del Hombre** (Museum of the History of Man). It won't take you long to visit this anthropology museum, where human development is explained from a Latin-American perspective. ✉ *Tres de Febrero 1370–8,* ☎ *11/4782-7251.* ✆ *Free.* ⊙ *Weekdays 10–6.*

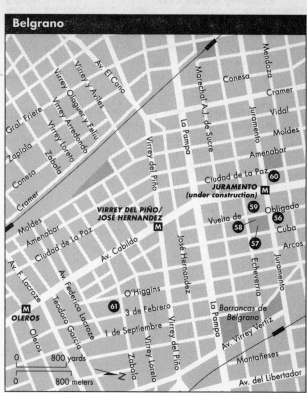

Belgrano

Mercado, **60**

Museo de Arte
Española
Enrique
Larreta, **56**

Museo
Histórico
Sarmiento, **57**

Museo
Nacional del
Hombre, **61**

Parroquia de
Nuestra Señora
de la
Inmaculata
Concepción, **59**

Plaza Manuel
Belgrano, **58**

⑤⑨ Parroquia de Nuestra Señora de la Inmaculada Concepción (Our Lady of the Immaculate Conception Church). This beautiful, brightly colored church was modeled after Rome's Pantheon. ✉ *Vuelta de Obligado 2042,* ☎ *11/4783–8008,* ⊙ *Mon.–Sat. 7:30–noon and 4–8:30, Sun. 7:30–1:30 and 4–9:15.*

⑤⑧ Plaza Manuel Belgrano. This square, named after General Belgrano, the War of Independece hero, is the site of a bustling art fair on weekends. During the week it's a simple city plaza, with a little playground filled with families and schoolchildren.

3 Dining

ALL KINDS OF INTERNATIONAL FARE can be found in Buenos Aires, but most common are *parrillas*—restaurants serving grilled meat. These vary from upscale eateries to local spots. Different cuts of beef are available here, as are chicken, sausage, and grilled cheese (*provoleta*). Meat dishes are generally accompanied by french fries and salad. Many restaurants also serve pasta (often homemade).

Cafés are a big part of Buenos Aires culture, and those in good locations are always busy, from breakfast to long after dinner. Some, called *confiterías*, have a wider selection of food—open-face sandwiches, grilled ham and cheese, "triples" (three-decker clubs filled with ham, cheese, tomatoes, olives, eggs, and onion), sandwiches made on *medias lunas* (croissants), salads, and desserts.

Argentina is basically a steak-and-potatoes country. The beef is so good, most Argentines see little reason to eat anything else, though pork, lamb, and chicken are tasty alternatives and *chivito* (kid), when in season, is outstanding. Nothing, however, can duplicate the indescribable flavor of a lean, tender, 3-inch thick *bife de lomo* (filet mignon) or a *bife de chorizo* (like New York steak, but double the size). *Jugoso* (juicy) means medium rare, *vuelta y vuelta* (flipped back and forth) means rare, and *vivo por adentro* (alive inside) is barely warm in the middle. Argentines like their meat *bién cocido* (well cooked). *Carne asado* (roasted meat) usually means grilled *a la parrilla* (on a grill over hot coals), but it can also be baked in an oven or *asado* (slowly roasted at an outdoor barbecue). Here, the meat is attached to an *asador* (metal spit), which is stuck in the ground aslant on a bed of hot coals. A *tira de asado* (strip of rib roast), skewered on its own spit, often accompanies the asado.

A *parrillada mixta* (mixed grill) is the quintessential Argentine meal for two or more. Families gather for noon *parrilladas* (grills) in restaurants and backyards across the country. They choose from different cuts of beef, *mollejas* (sweetbreads), *chichulínes* (intestines), *salchichas* (long, thin sausages), *morcillas* (blood sausages), chicken, and *chorizos* (thick, spicy pork-and-beef sausages)—terrific on french bread slathered with *chimichurri* sauce (oil, garlic, and salt) and items such as crushed red pepper, chopped cilantro, parsley, oregano, or tomatoes. All these morsels sizzle on a portable grill delivered to your table along with french fries cooked on a hot skillet (not submerged in oil).

Beyond beef, many Argentine dishes are influenced by other cultures. Pasta, pizza, and Italian specialties are on every menu in almost all restaurants. A *milanesa* (breaded veal cutlet) is a good quick snack, even better *a la neopolitana* with melted mozzarella cheese and tomato sauce. Fish has never been a favored dish in this meat-loving country.

Argentines also tend to ignore vegetables, except for salads, which usually include shredded carrots, tomatoes, onions, cabbage, and cucumbers. Ask for *aceite de olivo* (olive oil) or you'll get corn oil for your salad. Not to be missed, when available, is the white asparagus that grows south of Buenos Aires. Vegetables and fruits are fresh, crisp, and flavorful in their seasons—no need for hothouse assistance in this country.

A welcome sight on the dessert menu is *ensalada de fruta* (fruit salad—sometimes fresh, sometimes canned). *Dulce de leche* is a sweet caramel sauce served on pancakes, in pastries, on cookies (*alfajores*), and on ice cream.

Given the high consumption of beef rather than fish, Argentines understandably drink *vino tinto* (red wine). Malbec and cabernet are the most popular. If you prefer *vino blanco* (white wine), try vintages from Mendoza and lesser known wineries farther north: La Rioja and Salta. Here the Torrontés grape thrives. This varietal produces a dry white with an overwhelming, unforgettable bouquet that has been a consistent prize winner in recent competitions in Germany and France. A popular summer cooler is *clericot,* a white version of sangría (also available in many restaurants), made with strawberries, peaches, oranges, or whatever fruits are in season.

CATEGORY	COST*
$$$$	over $35
$$$	$25–$35
$$	$15–$25
$	$5–$15
¢	under $5

*per person for an appetizer, entrée, and dessert, excluding
tax, tip, and beverages*

Belgrano

Italian

$$$ ✕ **La Fornarina.** This cozy basement eatery in the heart of
★   the fashionable Belgrano district is worth the $8 cab ride
from El Centro. The homemade pastas and desserts are ex-
cellent. Traditional Argentine cuisine is also available. ⊠
Vuelta de Obligado, ☎ *11/4783–4904. AE, DC, MC, V.
Subte: Estación Juramento.*

Pan-Asian

$$–$$$ ✕ **Tao Tao.** Porteños come from all over the city for the lo-
★   cally influenced Japanese and Chinese fare at Tao Tao. It's
also not uncommon to see ambassadors and visiting dig-
nitaries from Asian countries here. The surroundings are
formal Chinese; the multilingual staff is excellent. As an ap-
petizer, sample the crunchy *empanaditas* (an Argentine ver-
sion of spring rolls), and for a main dish, opt for the lobster
rice or the Japanese salad. ⊠ *Av. Cabildo 1418,* ☎ *11/4783–
5806. Reservations essential on Sat. AE, V. Closed Mon.
Subte: Estación Jose Hernandez/Virrey del Piño.*

La Boca

Argentine

$–$$ ✕ **El Obrero.** When the rock band U2 played in Buenos
Aires in 1998, they asked to be taken to the most traditional
Argentine restaurant in the city—and this is where they were
brought. A bustling hole-in-the-wall, it serves consistently good
steaks, sweetbreads, sausages, and grilled chicken. The stark
walls and cheap (even by Argentine standards) wine make
it clear that you're not in a jacket-and-tie kind of place, but
the food is cheap, fast, and always enjoyable. Note: Some
cab drivers may not want to take you to the area around this

restaurant; also you should expect a wait. ⊠ *Augustín R. Caffarena 64,* ☎ *11/4363–9912. No credit cards. Closed Jan.*

Cabalito

Spanish

$$ ✕ **Los Chanchitos.** This is a typical cantina, complete with hanging hams and a noisy crowd. Dishes are abundant, often enough for two. The smoky atmosphere and flowing drinks make this a place to spend an evening. ⊠ *Angel Gallardo 601,* ☎ *11/4857–3738. MC, V.*

El Centro

Argentine

$$$ ✕ **Las Nazarenas.** Across the street from the Sheraton, in a two-story Spanish colonial–style building with wrought-iron sconces and potted ferns, this parrilla is a favorite lunch stop for businesspeople. Meat is the order of the day, whether grilled steaks, brochettes, or chivito. For an appetizer, order the *matambre* (a meat dish, typically served cold, made from pounded meat layered with hard-boiled egg and spices, rolled up like a log, and sliced), the grilled provolone cheese sprinkled with oregano, or the delicious empanadas. ⊠ *Reconquista 1132,* ☎ *11/4312–5559. AE, DC, MC, V. Estación San Martín.*

$$$ ✕ **Tierra de los Cocineros.** An unusual mix of Argentine fare
★ like *lomito* (a cut of beef similar to filet mignon, often served thinly sliced as a sandwich) and *ñoquis* (gnocchi) and international dishes such as pad thai and curry chicken are available at this bright, modern restaurant. It's extremely popular with a business-lunch crowd, so it can take a while to get a table at midday. ⊠ *Juncal 810,* ☎ *11/4393–2010. AE, DC, MC, V. Closed Sun. Subte: Estación Plaza San Martín.*

$$$ ✕ **Tomo Uno.** In the Hotel Panamericano (☞ Chapter 4), this restaurant has some dishes that aren't typically found in Buenos Aires restaurants—such as the tasty lamb with herbs, garnished with Spanish potatoes and spinach, and the trout with lemon sauce and roasted almonds. If you're in town on Easter or Christmas Eve, this is a good place

Buenos Aires Dining

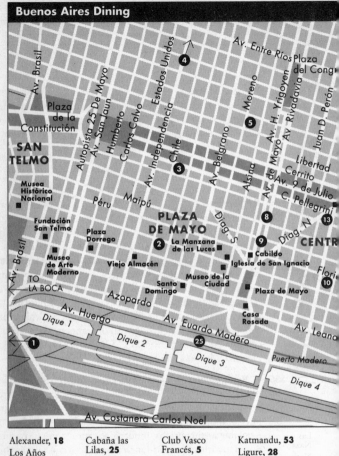

Las Nazarenas, **23**	Plaka, **52**	Syrian Club, **38**
Novecento, **43**	Los Platitos, **58**	Taberna Baska, **3**
El Obrero, **1**	Plaza Hotel Grill, **22**	Tao Tao, **50**
El Palacio de la Papa Frita, **12**	La Querencia, **26**	Tierro de los Cocineros, **27**
Pedemonte, **9**	Río Alba, **41**	Tomo Uno, **14**
La Pergola, **17**	Rosa Negra, **55**	Veracruz, **7**
Petit Paris Café, **29**	San Babila, **36**	Yin Yang, **15**
Pippo, **6**	El Sanjuanino, **31**	
Pizza Cero, **48**	Sensu, **11**	

Map key: **AE** American Express Office

to come. ⊠ *Carlos Pellegrini 525,* ☎ *11/4348–5000. Reservations essential. AE, DC, MC, V. Closed Sun. No lunch Sat. Subte: Estación 9 de Julio, Carlos Pellegrini.*

$$ ✕ **El Palacio de la Papa Frita.** A good place for a quick meal before or after a movie, this family establishment is always packed. There's lots of good, solid food—everything from chicken salad to spaghetti to grilled steak and fries. ⊠ *Lavalle 735,* ☎ *11/4393–5849. AE, DC, MC, V. Subte: Estación Lavalle.*

$–$$ ✕ **Melo** In Barrio Norte, a neighborhood bordering El
★   Centro and La Recoleta, Melo serves up traditional steaks, salads, and pastas. Portions are huge—usually big enough for two, and the friendly atmosphere makes up for the sparse decor. Particularly good is the brochette of meat and vegetables. ⊠ *Pachero de Melo,* ☎ *11/4801–4251. No credit cards.*

$–$$ ✕ **Pippo.** This is the place to go for *estofado* (a traditional meat sauce) and pasta as well as lomito and french fries. The food is inexpensive, the atmosphere is relaxed, and you're allowed to linger over your food as long as you like. ⊠ *Paraná 356,* ☎ *11/4374–6365. No credit cards. No dinner Sun. Subte: Estación Tribunales.*

$ ✕ **La Querencia.** This country-style restaurant serves various types of empanadas and tamales as well as rich local soups and stews such as the traditional *locro* (a stew of hard corn, cooked slowly for days). Seating is on stools, but you can also carry out. There are two locations in El Centro. ⊠ *Esmeralda 1392,* ☎ *11/4822–4644. Subte: Estación San Martín;* ⊠ *Junin 1304,* ☎ *11/4393–3202. Subte: Estación Facultad de Medicina. No credit cards. Closed Sun.*

Cafés

$ ✕ **Florida Garden.** Sit elbow to elbow along the 20-ft bar or in the sitting room upstairs, and enjoy afternoon tea or some of the richest hot chocolate in the city. ⊠ *Florida 889, near the Plaza San Martín,* ☎ *11/4312–7902. No credit cards. Subte: Estación Plaza San Martín.*

$ ✕ **Gran Café Tortoni.** Dating from 1858, this confitería is
★   the oldest in town. Its wooden tables, original artwork, and decorated ceilings are reminiscent of a faded, glorious past. Carlos Gardel, one of Argentina's most famous tango stars, writer José Luis Borges, Argentinian presidents, and many

visiting dignitaries and intellectuals have had coffee here. On weekend nights there's a tango show (reservations essential). ✉ *Near Plaza de Mayo at Av. de Mayo 829,* ☎ *11/ 4342–4328. AE, MC, V. Subte: Estación Avenida de Mayo.*

$ ★ ✕ **Ideal.** Charming and a little bit tattered, this café makes you feel like you've gone back in time. Not only can you come here for coffee, but you can also take beginning tango lessons and see experts perform on Tuesday and Friday nights. Some of the 1998 film *The Tango Lesson* was shot here. Unlike the Gran Café Tortoni (☞ *above*), it's fairly easy to get a table here; just beware the grouchy waiters who pretend not to understand tourists. ✉ *Suipacha 384, near corner of Av. Corrientes,* ☎ *11/4326–0521. AE, MC, V. Subte: Estación 9 de Julio.*

$ ✕ **Petit Paris Café.** The crystal chandeliers and marble tabletops make this place feel especially like a Parisian café. A variety of coffees are served, as are tasty salads and sandwiches. ✉ *Av. Santa Fe 774,* ☎ *11/4312–5885. AE. Subte: Estación Plaza San Martín*

Continental

$$$$ ✕ **La Pergola.** On the third floor of the Hotel Libertador Kempinski, this restaurant serves mouthwatering appetizers such as salmon bisque and flavorful entrées, including pasta; grilled steak; and sole with shrimp, artichoke hearts, shallots, capers, asparagus, and white wine sauce. ✉ *Maipú and Av. Córdoba,* ☎ *11/4322–8800 or 11/4322–6622. Reservations essential. Jacket and tie. AE, DC, MC, V. Subte: Estación Plaza San Martín.*

$$$$ ★ ✕ **Plaza Hotel Grill.** Wrought-iron lamps and fans hang from the high ceilings, and original Dutch delft porcelain tiles decorate the walls at this favorite spot of executives and politicians. There's an extensive wine list and a Continental menu with excellent steak, fish dishes such as salmon with basil and red wine, and quail stuffed with foie gras and grapes. ✉ *Florida 1005, in the Plaza Hotel,* ☎ *11/4318–3000 or 11/4313–7403. Reservations essential. Jacket and tie. AE, DC, MC, V. Subte: Estación San Martín.*

English

$$$ ✕ **Alexander.** Come here for the food, not the decor. The rack of lamb—not a common sight on Argentine menus— melts in the mouth, and the purées of vegetables such as

sweet potato, squash, and pumpkin are delicious. Lunch is usually very busy. ⊠ *San Martín 774,* ☎ *11/4311–2878. Reservations essential* . *AE, DC, MC, V. Closed Sun. Subte: Estación Plaza San Martín.*

$$$ ✕ **Down Town Matías.** Tucked behind the Plaza Hotel on the ground floor of a modern high-rise, this restaurant serves such typical English fare as lamb stew and chicken pie in a chummy, publike atmosphere. ⊠ *San Martín 979,* ☎ *11/4312–9844. AE, DC, MC, V. No credit cards. Closed Sun. Subte: Estación Plaza San Martín.*

French

$$$$ ✕ **Catalinas.** Superb seafood and game dishes await you
★   at this French restaurant that resembles a country inn. The lobster tail on fresh eggs, with caviar and cream, and the *pejerrey* (a small freshwater fish) stuffed with king-crab mousse are particularly savory. The dining room is packed wall to wall with businesspeople at lunch, but it draws a more varied crowd at night. Several fixed-price menus make this gourmet's delight easier on the pocket, but beware—Catalinas's wines and desserts can double the price of your meal. ⊠ *Reconquista 875,* ☎ *11/4313–0182. Reservations essential. Jacket and tie. AE, DC, MC, V. Closed Sun. Subte: Estación Florida.*

$$ ✕ **Ligure.** French cuisine adapted to Argentine tastes is the specialty here. You can get dishes such as thistles au gratin as well as the more standard steak au poivre with brandy sauce. The dessert pancakes are a must. ⊠ *Juncal 855,* ☎ *11/4394–8226. AE, MC, V.*

$ ✕ **Bonpler.** If you're looking for a quick meal, come here for Argentine-style French fast food (seating is available): salads, sandwiches, croissants, muffins, and coffee. ⊠ *Florida 481, at Lavalle,* ☎ *11/4325–9900. No credit cards. Closed Sun. Subte: Estación Florida.*

Japanese

$ ✕ **Sensu.** Eat in or take out your food at this Japanese restaurant. The food is good—especially the salmon (there are also shrimp, beef, and chicken dishes, though no sushi)—and the mixed vegetables that come with every dish are a welcome change from the solitary steak plates served in most Argentine restaurants. ⊠ *Florida 528,* ☎ *11/4393–9595. No credit cards.*

Finally, a travel companion that doesn't snore on the plane or eat all your peanuts.

When traveling, your MCI WorldCom Card is the best way to keep in touch. Our operators speak your language, so they'll be able to connect you back home—no matter where your travels take you. Plus, your MCI WorldCom Card is easy to use, and even earns you frequent flyer miles every time you use it. When you add in our great rates, you get something even more valuable: peace-of-mind. So go ahead. Travel the world. MCI WorldCom just brought it a whole lot closer.

You can even sign up today at www.mci.com/worldphone or ask your operator to make a collect call to 1-410-314-2938.

EASY TO CALL WORLDWIDE

1 Just dial the WorldPhone access number of the country you're calling from.
2 Dial or give the operator your MCI WorldCom Card number.
3 Dial or give the number you're calling.

Argentina	
To call using Telefonica	0-800-222-6249
To call using Telecom	0-800-555-1002
Brazil	000-8012
France ◆	0-800-99-0019
Ireland	1-800-55-1001
United Kingdom	
To call using BT	0800-89-0222
To call using CWC	0500-89-0222
United States	1-800-888-8000

For your complete WorldPhone calling guide, dial the WorldPhone access number for the country you're in and ask the operator for Customer Service. In the U.S. call 1-800-431-5402.

◆ Public phones may require deposit of coin or phone card for dial tone.

EARN FREQUENT FLYER MILES

The first thing you need overseas is the one thing you forget to pack.

FOREIGN CURRENCY DELIVERED OVERNIGHT

Chase Currency To Go® delivers foreign currency to your home by the next business day*

It's easy—before you travel, call 1-888-CHASE84 for delivery of any of 75 currencies

Delivery is free with orders of $500 or more

Competitive rates— without exchange fees

You don't have to be a Chase customer—you can pay by Visa® or MasterCard®

CHASE

THE RIGHT RELATIONSHIP IS EVERYTHING.®

1•888•CHASE84
www.chase.com

Pizza

$$ ✗ Filo. ★ Come here for the flat-bread pizza, the extensive drink list, and the great party atmosphere. It's definitely not the place for a quiet, relaxing meal, as the popular bar is packed all the time. ✉ *San Martín 975,* ☎ *11/4311–0312. AE, MC, V. Subte: Estación Plaza San Martín.*

$$ ✗ Memorabilia. The young and fashionable flock to this trendy restaurant-bar where the walls are painted orange and yellow, music videos are shown, and pizza is made in a purple-painted brick oven. Besides creative pizzas, you can also get pasta, salads, and sandwiches. Often there's live music or dancing after 10 PM. ✉ *Maipú 761,* ☎ *11/ 4322–7630. AE, DC, MC, V. Subte: Estación San Martín.*

Spanish

$$$ ✗ Veracruz. This old-fashioned restaurant has carefully prepared Spanish-style seafood dishes served by staid, seasoned waiters. Especially delicious is the *cazuela* (seafood stew with clams, shrimp, octopus, scallops, and lobster). ✉ *Uruguay 538,* ☎ *11/4371–1413. MC, V. Closed Sun.*

$$ ✗ Club Vasco Francés. In an old racquet club, this spacious, spruced-up dining room is one of the few places in Buenos Aires where you can get frogs' legs. Seafood is flown in from Spain especially for homesick Basque diners. ✉ *Moreno 1370,* ☎ *11/4383–5021. AE, V. Closed Sun.*

Vegetarian

$ ✗ Yin-Yang. Yin-Yang caters to health-conscious vegetarians with a well-balanced menu of large, tasty plates of brown rice, fresh vegetables, tofu, and vegetable tarts. ✉ *Paraguay 858,* ☎ *11/4311–7798. No credit cards. Subte: Estación 9 de Julio.*

Costanera (Río de la Plata)

Argentine

$$$ ✗ Los Años Locos. ★ Locals flock to this restaurant, along the banks of the Río de la Plata, for long lunches and late-night steak dinners, served in a friendly, low-key atmosphere. It's not uncommon to be finishing up your steak at 1 AM and to see a group waiting for your table. Portions are more than generous—for most cuts of meat, order a half portion, unless you intend to share. The decor isn't noteworthy—it's basically a lot of tables, packed into a huge room that's always full, but you won't even notice after you've taken your first bite. After dinner you can cross the street to see the river at night, though it's not recommended that you stray too far from the restaurant. ⊠ *Rafael Obligado and La Pampa,* ☏ *11/4784–8681. AE, DC, V.*

$–$$ ✕ **Los Platitos.** At this no-frills restaurant, jovial waiters serve
★ up traditional Argentine fare such as blood sausage and sweetbreads with pasta and grilled provolone. Because it's on the Costanera (the river drive), you'll need to take a taxi or drive. ⊠ *Rafael Obligado and La Pampa, on the Costanera,* ☏ *no phone. AE, DC, V.*

Italian

$$$ ✕ **Clo-Clo.** Enjoy the view of the Río de la Plata as you feast on grilled beef and piles of *papas fritas* (french fries). *Trucha Capri* (trout in cream sauce with prawns) is a good way to whet your appetite. ⊠ *Costanera Norte and La Pampa,* ☏ *11/4788–0487. AE, DC, MC, V.*

Palermo

American

$ ✕ **Big Momma.** Argentina's version of a deli has a little bit of everything you'd expect (except pickles), such as made-to-order sandwiches, hot pastrami, bagels and lox, and even knishes. ⊠ *Migueletes and Matienzo,* ☏ *11/4772–0926. AE, DC, MC, V.*

Argentine

$$$ ✕ **Novecento.** This bistro has an American theme—New
★ York City street signs hang on the walls and the menu is in English and Spanish (in fact, there's also a Novecento in New York City's SoHo). Yet the food, atmosphere, and crowd are all chic Porteño. The candlelit tables are close together, which makes for intimate seating. The beef salad, a pyramid of alternating layers of green salad, steak, and french fries, is especially good. In summer there's outdoor dining. ⊠ *Báez 199,* ☏ *11/4778–1900. V. Subte: Estación Palermo.*

$$$ ✕ **Río Alba.** Stacked wine bottles, hanging hams, and sports-related memorabilia form the backdrop to such dishes as grilled tuna, salmon, and trout; or try the juicy, lean pork with lemon slices and shoestring potatoes. Right by the American Embassy, it's a noisy hangout for American expats. ✉ *Cerviño 4499,* ☎ *11/4773–9508. AE, DC, MC, V. Subte: Estación Palermo.*

$$–$$$ ✕ **Club del Vino.** With its wine cellar, wine museum, and wine boutique, this is paradise if you love wine. The prix fixe wine taster's menu includes milanesa with sweet potatoes and flan, accompanied by merlot, Malbec, and cabernet. ✉ *Cabrera 4737,* ☎ *11/4833–0048.* ☉ *No lunch. AE, DC, MC, V. Subte: Estación Palermo.*

$ ✕ **Ña Serapia.** Tasty tamales and locro as well as inexpensive wine make this a perfect quick stop in Palermo. The place is small, and the atmosphere is no-frills, but the food is consistently good. It's also one of the few restaurants with an Argentine menu that doesn't focus specifically on grilled meat. ✉ *Av. Las Heras 3357,* ☎ *11/4801–5307. No credit cards.*

Greek

$$ ✕ **Plaka.** Chef Lefteris Gakis prepares such traditional Greek fare as moussaka and grape leaves. Service is friendly—you're welcomed with a glass of Greek retsina. Concerts of traditional Greek music and dance are held on weekends. Note that the restaurant is sometimes closed for lunch, so it's a good idea to call ahead. ✉ *Arevalo 2725,* ☎ *11/4777–6051. V.*

Indian

$$$–$$$$ ✕ **Katmandu.** This cozy, off-the-beaten-path spot north of Palermo has eclectic Hindu art and two floors of Indian wares. The Indian food—especially the curries and breads—is some of the best in Buenos Aires. The crowd is primarily made up of expats living in Argentina and yuppie Porteños. ✉ *Cordoba 3547,* ☎ *11/4963–1122. AE, DC, MC, V. Closed Sun.*

Mexican

$–$$ ✕ **Cielito Lindo.** This Mexican cantina is a great reason to visit Palermo Viejo. The atmosphere is festive, with colorful Mexican decorations all over the walls. The food focuses on beans, rice, and spicy meats and the mixed drinks are surprisingly good for Buenos Aires (though the margaritas are definitely small by American standards). ⊠ *El Salvador 4999, at Thames,* ☎ *11/4832–8054. No credit cards. Closed Sun. No lunch.*

Middle Eastern

$$ ✕ **Asociación Cultural Armenia.** Ex-generals and future presidents can be found enjoying extraordinary Armenian fare alongside moguls of the city's powerful Armenian community in this rather institutional-looking Palermo Viejo club. The hummus, tabbouleh, and stuffed eggplant are authentic and well prepared. ⊠ *Armenia 1366,* ☎ *11/4771–0016. AE, DC, MC, V. Closed Mon. and Feb. No lunch Tues.–Sat.; no dinner Sat.*

Pizza

$$ ✕ **Morelia.** In the up-and-coming neighborhood of Las Cañitas is one of the best places in the city serving pizza cooked on a grill. After your meal, head across the street to one of the many trendy bars in the area. ⊠ *Báez 260,* ☎ *11/4772–0329. AE, DC, MC, V. No lunch. Subte: Estación Palermo.*

$$ ✕ **Pizza Cero.** New Age music, outdoor tables, and a dining room filled with fresh plants and flowers set the tone at this popular, upscale pizza parlor. The pizzas have crisp crusts and mozzarella cheese with an array of toppings, including eggplant, ham, and pineapple. Tasty salads and empanadas are also available. ⊠ *Cerviño 3701,* ☎ *11/4803–3449. V.*

Thai

$$$ ✕ **Lotus neo Thai.** At this enchanting Thai restaurant, colorful flower lamps reach for the ceiling, and glowing candles bob in carefully placed bowls. Excellent dishes include red curried beef in coconut milk with pumpkin and basil leaves, fried coconut shrimp with sweet and sour tamarind sauce, and stir-fried rice vermicelli with minced shrimp, chicken, and pork. The fruit drinks are delicious but can make your bill add up. ⊠ *Ortega y Gasset 1782,* ☎ *11/4771–4449. AE, MC. No lunch. Subte: Estación Palermo.*

Plaza de Mayo

Argentine

$$–$$$ ✕ **Calle de los Angeles.** The name of this restaurant, Street of the Angels, accurately depicts the decor (made to look like you're outside on the street) in this fun but somewhat touristy spot. Tables line both walls of the long, narrow dining room, a winding brick path runs down the middle, and tree branches hang overhead, which makes you feel as if you are dining alfresco somewhere in Spain. But the food is well-prepared and artfully served Argentine parrilla. ✉ *Chile 318,* ☏ *11/4361–8822. No credit cards.*

Continental

$$ ✕ **Pedemonte.** The menu is extensive and the dishes well prepared at this Continental restaurant. The three-course fixed-price menu includes such items as *pascualina de alcauciles* (artichoke pie) and pepper steak. ✉ *Av. de Mayo 676,* ☏ *11/4331–7179. Reservations essential. Jacket and tie. AE, DC, MC, V. Closed Sat. No dinner Sun. Subte: Estación Avenida de Mayo.*

Spanish

$$ ✕ **Taberna Baska.** Old-world decor and efficient service are hallmarks of this busy, no-nonsense Spanish restaurant. Try such dishes as *chiripones en su tinta* (a variety of squid in ink). ✉ *Chile 980,* ☏ *11/4334–0903. AE, DC, MC, V. Closed Mon. No dinner Sun.*

Puerto Madero

Along the banks of the Río de la Plata in Puerto Madero, a string of restaurants line the shore, where Argentines flock for slow lunches and late-night steak dinners.

Argentine

$$$$ ✕ **Cabaña las Lilas.** Presidents, movie stars, and Porteños
★ come here for the best meat in Buenos Aires. In fact, the restaurant has its own *estancia* (ranch) where it raises cattle for its grilled lomito and *cuadrillo* (beef cheeks). The wine cellar is well stocked with superb Argentine wines (try the Catena Zapata). Service is impeccable. If you have to wait

long for a table, as you undoubtedly will, enjoy a glass of champagne in the cigar bar. ⊠ *Av. Dávila 516,* ☎ *11/ 4313–1336. AE, DC, V.*

La Recoleta

La Recoleta's competition for fashionable dining is right here at the port. Quickly becoming one of the most chic places to be seen, restaurants can't open fast enough to keep up with the Saturday-evening customer demand. Take a walk along the dock (during a mealtime to witness the true flavor of the area), mix with the diners, and enjoy the views of the Río de la Plata.

Argentine

$$$$ ✕ **Harper's.** A fashionable lunch and dinner spot, Harper's is popular with a cross section of locals—from yuppies to businesspeople to neighborhood folks. They come here to enjoy tender steak and a hearty plate of pasta as well as a traditional favorite, *cordero del diablo* (a tangy lamb dish). Paintings by local artists hang on the walls. ⊠ *R. M. Ortíz 1763,* ☎ *11/4801–7140. AE, MC, V.*

$$ ✕ **Munich Recoleta.** This jam-packed place has been a fa-
★ vorite gathering spot for almost 40 years. The basic fare consists of great steak, creamed spinach, and shoestring potatoes, all served quickly and in generous portions. The lively atmosphere attracts young and old alike. Arrive early if you don't want to wait. ⊠ *R. M. Ortíz 1879,* ☎ *11/4804–3981. Reservations not accepted. No credit cards.*

$ ✕ **El Sanjuanino.** Empanadas and other traditional fare from the Andes are made at this long-established spot. Though you can get a quick bite here, it's primarily a take-out place. ⊠ *Posadas 1515,* ☎ *11/4804–2909. No credit cards. Closed Mon.*

Café

$ ✕ **La Biela.** This La Recoleta café is a popular local spot for sipping espressos, gossiping, and people-watching. Although there are tables inside, where the decor is Paris-inspired, the outdoor tables are the place to be in warm weather. ⊠ *Quintana and Junin. V.*

Continental

$$$–$$$$ ✕ **Clark's.** Deer heads hang from the dark wood panels, overlooking red-checkered tables at this Continental restaurant. Though the chefs are ambitious and innovative, they sometimes miss their mark. So stick with Clark's traditional specialties, such as pasta with creamy mushroom sauce or grilled meat. The fixed-price menus, which include four courses and wine, are a good deal. ⊠ *R. M. Ortíz 1777,* ☎ *11/4801–9502. AE, DC, MC, V.*

Eclectic

$$ ✕ **Mora X.** The handsome wooden bar, rich artwork, and high-windowed ceiling create an old-world, librarylike ambience. The five large paintings lining the main dining room wall represent, in order, the marina, the tango, the circus, the hunt, and the forest, and are often a point of discussion for diners. Enjoy delightful dishes such as grilled sirloin with cheddar sauce and mushrooms or sole with lemon sauce; profiteroles with raspberry sauce make a fine finish. ⊠ *Vicente López 2152,* ☎ *11/4803–0261. Reservations essential. AE, DC, MC, V.*

French

$$$$ ✕ **La Bourgogne.** Argentina's only truly gourmet estab-
★ lishment is in the Alvear Palace Hotel (☞ Chapter 4) and is generally considered the city's best—and one of the most expensive—restaurants in town. In the elegant dining room complete with white tablecloths and fresh roses, the sophisticated waitstaff brings you complimentary hors d'oeuvres as you peruse the menu of delicacies such as foie gras, rabbit, escargots, chateaubriand, and *côte de veau* (veal steak). ⊠ *Alvear 1891,* ☎ *11/4804–4031. Reservations essential. Jacket and tie. AE, DC, MC, V.*

Italian

$$$–$$$$ ✕ **San Babila.** This trattoria is one of the city's most popular Italian restaurants. *Pappardelle al pesto* (butterfly pasta in a pesto sauce) and *tortelloni di zucca* (oversize tortellini with pumpkin filling) are good bets, and the fixed-price menus give you more options. ⊠ *R. M. Ortíz 1815,* ☎ *11/4802–8981. AE, DC, MC, V.*

Japanese

$$$$ ✕ **Midori.** This Japanese restaurant and sushi bar in the Caesar Park Hotel (☞ Chapter 4) is brightly lighted, modern, and clean. Try the *teppanyaki* dishes—prime cuts of meat, fish, and seafood grilled right at your table. ✉ *Posadas 1232,* ☎ *11/4819–1100. Reservations essential. AE, DC, MC, V. No lunch. Closed Mon.*

Middle Eastern

$$$ ✕ **Syrian Club.** The breathtaking second-floor restaurant at the Syrian Club has a curved double staircase leading up to the third floor and a welcoming lobby bar on the entrance level. Come here for a superb Middle Eastern buffet with such items as hummus, stuffed grape leaves, and lamb. Belly dancers entertain and coffee-ground readers predict fortunes. ✉ *At Ayacucho and Melo. AE, V.*

San Isidro

Argentine

$$$$
★ ✕ **Rosa Negra.** Across from the San Isidro racetrack in the loft of a former horse stable, Rosa Negra serves Argentine parrilla and Italian cuisine to a sophisticated crowd. Try the traditionally prepared meats such as the lomito or the seafood ravioli. Be prepared to wait for a table—over an hour on Saturday—there's free champagne and plenty of people-watching to make it entertaining. ✉ *Dardo Rocha 1918,* ☎ *11/4717–2685. AE, V.*

4 Lodging

BUENOS AIRES HAS A VARIETY of fine hotels. Some of the more expensive ones were built for the 1978 World Cup, while others opened at the turn of the 20th century or even before. It's important to remember, however, that you're not in the United States (or Canada or England) and that where you stay is part of the adventure. So while some things may be hard to understand or tolerate (why aren't there screens on the windows, for instance?), try to stay flexible. With the exception of the top luxury hotels, most establishments have a small, family-run feel, with all the charming quirks that that entails.

Most rooms have a bidet, but not every room has a television. In many of the smaller hotels, it's not possible to make a direct-dial long-distance call from your room—you must either use a phone in the lobby or call the front desk to ask for a long-distance line. Don't expect to see such amenities as ice makers or vending machines.

In addition to the prices quoted, a 21% tax is generally added. Check-in time is usually after 3 PM, and check-out time is usually before noon, though these times are more flexible in smaller hotels.

CATEGORY	COST*
$$$$	over $150
$$$	$100–$150
$$	$50–$100
$	$25–$50
¢	under $25

Prices are for a double room in high season, excluding taxes.

El Centro

$$$$ 🏨 **Claridge.** The public rooms of this stylish hotel, with their wood paneling and high ceiling, have a distinctly British feel. There's an Anglo-Argentine clientele to match. Rooms are done in shades of blue, with dark wood furnishings with bronze fittings. The health club and pool are nice pluses. ⊠ *Tucumán 535, 1049,* ☎ *11/4314–7700, 800/223–5652*

in the U.S., FAX *11/4314–8022. 155 rooms, 6 suites. Restaurant, bar, room service, pool, health club, concierge, business services, meeting rooms. AE, DC, MC, V.*

$$$$ ⊞ **El Conquistador.** This hotel, near Plaza San Martín, is popular with businesspeople. The wood paneling in the public rooms and the small art gallery in the lobby lend a cozy touch, and the cheerful restaurant serves breakfast and snacks. Large windows, flowered bedspreads, and light pink carpets brighten rooms. ⊠ *Suipacha 948, 1008,* ☎ *11/4328–3012,* FAX *11/4328–3252. 130 rooms, 14 suites. Restaurant, piano bar, massage, sauna, exercise room. AE, DC, MC, V. Subte: Estación San Martín.*

$$$$ ⊞ **Crillon.** Right across from Plaza San Martín, the Crillon was built in classic French style in 1948 and remodeled in 1995. Front rooms have beautiful views and are large and luminous. The lobby is stately and sedate, which may explain why this establishment appeals to provincial governors and the well-to-do from the interior. ⊠ *Av. Santa Fe 796, 1059,* ☎ *11/4310–2000 or 0800/84448,* FAX *11/4310–2020. 84 rooms, 12 suites. Restaurant, bar, in-room safes, room service, concierge, business services, meeting room. AE, DC, MC, V. Subte: Estación Plaza San Martín.*

$$$$ ⊞ **Inter-Continental.** One of Buenos Aires's newest luxury hotels, the Inter-Continental was designed with Argentina of the 1930s in mind. The elegant lobby, with marble, leather, bronze, and wood, leads to an outdoor terrace with a fountain. Rooms are adorned with large black armoires, marble-top nightstands, sleeper chairs, and black-and-white photos of Buenos Aires. The hotel's location in Monserrat, just above El Centro, is a mixed blessing—the neighborhood is quiet, but there's not much to do nearby. ⊠ *Moreno 809, 1091,* ☎ *11/4340–7100,* FAX *11/4340–7119. 315 rooms and suites. Restaurant, 2 bars, room service, indoor pool, health club, concierge, business services, meeting rooms, parking. AE, DC, MC, V.*

$$$$ ⊞ **Libertador Kempinski.** This European-style hotel near the banking district serves as the base for many visiting businesspeople. The lobby, with its marble floor, has a bar and is a good spot to rendezvous. Standard rooms are classic but petite; the pastel-shade deluxe rooms have walk-in closets, marble baths, and mahogany furnishings. ⊠ *Av. Córdoba 690, 1054,* ☎ *11/4322–8800,* FAX *11/4322–9703.*

197 rooms, 6 suites. Restaurant, bar, coffee shop, room service, indoor-outdoor pool, health club, concierge, meeting rooms, travel services. AE, DC, MC, V.

$$$$ 🏨 **Marriott Plaza Hotel.** One of the city's grandest hotels
★ is across from Plaza San Martín. Marriott has poured millions into the hotel since it was purchased in 1994. Crystal chandeliers and Persian carpets decorate the public rooms—the president of Argentina likes to entertain visiting dignitaries here. Some rooms have great bay windows overlooking the park; all are spacious and elegantly appointed. ✉ *Florida 1005, 1005,* ☎ *11/4318–3000, 800/228–9290 in the U.S.,* ℻ *11/4318–3008. 274 rooms, 38 suites. 2 restaurants, bar, café, in-room safes, room service, pool, health club, concierge, business services, meeting rooms. AE, DC, MC, V. Subte: Estación San Martín.*

$$$$ 🏨 **Sheraton Buenos Aires Hotel.** The headquarters of Sheraton's South American division, this huge hotel at the bottom of Plaza San Martín has a broad range of facilities. The standard-looking rooms have views of either the Río de la Plata or the British Clock Tower and park at Retiro. It's especially popular with American businesspeople and tour groups. In late 1996 the separate Park Tower, part of Sheraton's Luxury Group, was built next door with spacious, expensive rooms that have cellular phones, entertainment centers, and 24-hour butler service. ✉ *San Martín 1225, 1104,* ☎ *11/4318–9000, 800/325–3535 in the U.S.,* ℻ *11/4318–9353. 603 rooms, 29 suites. 4 restaurants, bar, coffee shop, pool, 2 tennis courts, health club, concierge, business services, meeting rooms, car rental, parking (fee). AE, DC, MC, V. Subte: Estación Retiro.*

$$$ 🏨 **Bisonte Hotel.** This hotel, on a popular shopping street, has a small, marble-floor lobby and an upstairs coffee shop overlooking a tree-lined square. Rooms are small, and the decor is on the stiff side, however. Breakfast is included in the rates. ✉ *Paraguay 1207, 1057,* ☎ *11/4816–5770,* ℻ *11/4816–5775. 87 rooms. Coffee shop, business services. AE, DC, MC, V. Subte: Estación 9 de Julio.*

$$$ 🏨 **Bisonte Palace Hotel.** This brightly lighted version of its sister establishment, the Bisonte Hotel (☞ *above*), is centrally located and popular with business travelers. Decor is standard—modern and comfortable—and you're well taken care of, though the atmosphere is a bit cold and formal. Because it's on a busy corner, rooms higher up are better bets for peace and quiet. Breakfast is included in the rate. ✉ *M. T. de Alvear 902, 1058,* ☎ *11/4328–4751,* FAX *11/4328–6476. 62 rooms. Coffee shop, room service. AE, DC, MC, V. Subte: Estación San Martín.*

$$$ 🛏 **Buenos Aires Bauen Hotel.** With its theater, auditorium, tango shows, and city tours, the Bauen is a beehive of activity. It's near the intersection of two noisy avenues lined with lively restaurants, cafés, movie houses, and theaters, so avoid the lower floors if you think you'll be bothered by the noise. ✉ *Av. Callao 360, 1022,* ☎ *11/4370–1600, 800/448–8355 in the U.S.,* FAX *11/4372–0315. 226 rooms, 28 suites. Restaurant, bar, coffee shop, refrigerators, room service, pool, barbershop, beauty salon, convention center. AE, DC, MC, V. Subte: Estación Callao.*

$$$ 🛏 **Carsson.** A long, mirrored corridor leads to the lobby, far from the sound of downtown traffic. An English atmosphere pervades—rooms have staid stripes of green and deep red and Louis XIV–style furniture and are larger than the average Buenos Aires hotel room; ask for one off the busy street. Service is first rate. ✉ *Viamonte 650, 1053,* ☎ *11/ 4322–3551,* FAX *11/4322–0158. 108 rooms, 9 suites. Bar, coffee shop, in-room safes, room service, nursery, laundry service, business services, meeting rooms, parking (fee). AE, DC, MC, V. Subte: Estación Lavalle.*

$$$ 🛏 **De las Américas.** In this modern residential hotel just off the shopping stretch of Avenida Santa Fe, the sunken lobby is drearily decorated. But rooms are comfortable and larger than you'd expect. The clientele consists mainly of South American tour groups and visitors from the provinces. The metro stop is close, but probably not close enough if you're carrying bags. ✉ *Libertad 1020, 1012,* ☎ *11/4816–3432,* FAX *11/4816–0418. 150 rooms, 15 suites. Coffee shop, room service. AE, DC, MC, V. Subte: Estación Tribunales.*

$$$ 🛏 **Gran Hotel Colón.** Near the Obelisk, off busy Avenida 9 de Julio, the shiny, modern Colón has suites with private patios; standard rooms, however, are shoe-box size. Airport buses leave from out front. ✉ *Av. Carlos Pellegrini 507, 1009,* ☎ *11/4320–3500, 800/448–8355 in the U.S.,* FAX *11/ 4320–3507. 183 rooms, 23 suites. Restaurant, bar, room service, pool. AE, DC, MC, V. Subte: Estación 9 de Julio.*

Buenos Aires Lodging

Alvear Palace Hotel, **22**

Bisonte Hotel, **25**

Bisonte Palace Hotel, **26**

Buenos Aires Bauen Hotel, **3**

Caesar Park, **21**

Carsson, **12**

Castelar Hotel, **4**

Claridge, **10**

El Conquistador, **28**

Constitución Palace Hotel, **1**

Crillon, **19**

De Las Américas, **24**

Gran Hotel Atlantic, **2**

Gran Hotel Colón, **8**

Gran Hotel Dora, **18**

Gran Hotel Hispano, **6**

Gran Hotel Orly, **14**

Hotel Alpino, **29**

Hotel Salles, **7**

Hotel Vicente Lopez, **30**

Inter-Continental, **5**

Lancaster, **11**

Libertador Kempinski, **13**

Marriott Plaza Hotel, **16**

Park Hyatt Buenos Aires, **20**

Plaza Francia, **23**

TO
PALERMO

Museo Nacional
de Arte Decorativo

Biblioteca
Nacional

Callao

LA RECOLETA

Av. Gral. Las Heras

Av. Pte. F. Alcorta

Plaza
Mitre

Av. Córdoba

M.T. De Alvear

Paraguay

Av. Santa Fe

Cementerio de
La Recoleta

Av. Pte. F. Quintana

Museo Nacional de Bellas Artes

Centro Cultural Recoleta

Teatro
Colón

Av. Alvear

Arenales

Juncal

Plaza
San
Martín

Palacio
San Martín

Av. Ant. Argentina

Av. Ramon S. Castillo

N

0   1 mile
0   2 km

KEY

[AE] American Express Office

\$\$\$ 🏨 **Posta Carretas.** This modern and very comfortable property has the atmosphere of a mountain inn. Wood paneling abounds, creating a coziness that contrasts with the bustle outside. Some of the brightly decorated rooms have hot tubs. ⊠ *Esmeralda 726, 1007,* ☎ *11/4322–8534,* FAX *11/4326–2277. 40 rooms, 11 suites. Bar, room service, pool, exercise room, sauna, business services. AE, DC, MC, V. Subte: Estación San Martín.*

\$\$\$ 🏨 **Principado.** Built for the World Cup in 1978, this hotel has reception areas with large windows and lots of light and a two-tier Spanish colonial–style lobby with leather couches. The highlight is the friendly coffee shop. Rooms are modern and comfortable. ⊠ *Paraguay 481, 1057,* ☎ *11/4313–3022,* FAX *11/4313–3952. 88 rooms. Coffee shop. AE, DC, MC, V. Subte: Estación San Martín.*

\$\$\$ 🏨 **Regente Palace.** The winding brass staircase, numerous mirrors, and neon lights in the lobby make you feel like you've entered a '70s casino or a Burt Reynolds movie. Yet rooms are pleasant if small and are decorated with black wood furniture and bedspreads and curtains in beige and rose. It's near Plaza San Martín on a block with several cafés and trendy shops. ⊠ *Suipacha 964, 1008,* ☎ *11/4328–6800,* FAX *11/4328–7460. 150 rooms, 6 suites. Restaurant, snack bar. AE, DC, MC, V. Subte: Estación San Martín.*

\$\$ 🏨 **Castelar Hotel.** Rooms have that rather institutional style associated with a business hotel; yet they're comfortable, and the lobby is small and inviting. The hotel spa has a Turkish-style bath—a rarity in Buenos Aires. It's an ideal place if you plan to focus on the Plaza de Mayo area. Breakfast is included in the rates. ⊠ *Av. de Mayo 1152, 1085,* ☎ *11/4383–5000,* FAX *11/4383–8388. 50 rooms. Bar, snack bar, spa, exercise room, laundry service, dry cleaning, meeting rooms. AE, MC, V. Subte: Estación Avenida de Mayo.*

\$\$ 🏨 **Gran Hotel Dora.** A cozy lobby with a small bar greets you at this old-fashioned hotel. Rooms are comfortable, elegant, and decorated in Louis XVI style. It caters primarily to Europeans and Argentines who want a Continental atmosphere. ⊠ *Maipú 963, 1006,* ☎ *11/4312–7391,* FAX *11/4313–8134. 96 rooms. Bar, snack bar, meeting rooms. AE, DC, MC, V. Subte: Estación San Martín.*

\$\$ 🏨 **Hotel Salles.** This quiet, central establishment is one of the few family-oriented hotels in the heart of the theater district. Rooms are adequate, the decor businesslike and institutional; personal service is a focus. ⊠ *Cerrito 208, 1010,* ☎ *11/4382–3962,* FAX *11/4382–0754. 80 rooms, 5 suites. Coffee shop. AE, DC, MC, V. Subte: Estación 9 de Julio.*

$$ ★ 🏨 **Lancaster.** The countess who decorated this traditional and central hotel made good use of her family heirlooms—old family portraits, marble pillars, and a 200-year-old clock grace the lobby. All rooms have antique mahogany furniture, and some have views of the port of Buenos Aires. ⊠ *Av. Córdoba 405, 1054,* ☎ *11/4312–4061,* FAX *11/4311–3021. 88 rooms, 16 suites. Restaurant, bar, room service, meeting rooms. AE, DC, MC, V. Subte: Estación Leandro N. Alem.*

$ 🏨 **Gran Hotel Atlantic.** If you're looking for inexpensive (if basic) rooms and friendly (though not very quick) service, this is the place for you. ⊠ *Castelli 45, 1031,* ☎ *11/4951–0081,* FAX *11/4951–0081. Bar, room service, parking. AE, DC, MC, V. Subte: Estación Plaza de Miserre.*

$ 🏨 **Gran Hotel Hispano.** The Spanish colonial architecture and small but charming rooms with flower motifs give this hotel a traditional yet friendly feel. Guests are primarily from neighboring Latin American countries. ⊠ *Av. de Mayo 861, 1084,* ☎ *11/4345–2020,* FAX *11/4345–5266. 60 rooms. Bar, breakfast room, ice cream parlor, laundry. AE, DC, MC, V. Subte: Estación Piedras.*

$ 🏨 **Gran Hotel Orly.** Off Calle Florida, the Orly draws Brazilian tourists and visitors from the interior. Although the entrance is impressive, rooms are plain and small and have noisy air-conditioners. The old-timer reception staff seems to be frozen in the previous century. But you can't beat it if you're looking for a clean, basic, inexpensive place to sleep. ⊠ *Paraguay 474, 1057,* ☎ *11/4312–5344,* FAX *11/4312–5344. 168 rooms, 8 suites. Bar, coffee shop. AE, DC, MC, V. Subte: Estación Facultad de Medicina.*

Palermo

$$ 🏨 **Hotel Alpino.** This hotel has functional if uninteresting rooms. The Parque Zoológico and the Jardín Botánico are within easy walking distance. Breakfast is included in the rates. ⊠ *Cabello 3318, 1425,* ☎ *11/4802–5151,* FAX *11/4802–5151. 35 rooms. Bar, in-room safes, parking. AE, DC, MC, V. Subte: Estación Plaza Italia.*

La Recoleta

$$$$ 🏨 **Alvear Palace Hotel.** Built in 1932 as a luxury apartment
★ building, the Alvear has since become the city's most elegant hotel and is often the site of receptions for visiting diplo-
mats and dignitaries. Rooms are done in French Empire–
style, in regal burgundy and deep blue, and have large windows, silk drapes, and feather beds. The hotel is convenient
to many museums and good restaurants. ✉ *Av. Alvear
1891, 1129,* ☏ *11/4808–2100 or 11/4804–7777, 800/
448–8355 in the U.S.,* ☎ *11/4804–0034. 100 rooms, 100
suites. Restaurant, coffee shop, lobby lounge, piano bar, tea
shop, indoor pool, health club, concierge, business services, meeting rooms. AE, DC, MC, V.*

$$$$ 🏨 **Caesar Park.** Opposite Patio Bullrich, this Westin-
operated hotel is near La Recoleta and Plaza San Martín.
The lavish, spacious rooms have tasteful fabrics, period
furniture, marble bathrooms, and good light, though
they're a bit generic when compared with other historic hotels. Upper floors have a panoramic view of the river. If
you're staying at the hotel, you have access (for a fee) to a
nearby 18-hole golf course. ✉ *Posadas 1232, 1011,* ☏
11/4819–1100, 800/228–3000 in the U.S., ☎ *11/4819–
1120. 172 rooms, 20 suites. 3 restaurants, bar, in-room
modem lines, room service, indoor pool, beauty salon,
health club, business services, meeting rooms. AE, DC,
MC, V.*

$$$$ 🏨 **Park Hyatt Buenos Aires.** On the edge of La Recoleta,
★ the luxurious Park Hyatt has a 13-floor marble tower and
an adjacent turn-of-the-20th-century mansion, with private
butler service for its handsome suites. This is where Madonna
stayed for two months during the filming of *Evita.* In addition to its million-dollar art collection, the hotel houses
a beautiful Roman-style pool, health club, and landscaped
garden. Guest rooms are the largest of any Buenos Aires
hotel, and outstanding service ensures many repeat visitors
(when you check in, the hotel staff sits down with you to
determine your needs). ✉ *Posadas 1086, 1011,* ☏ *11/
4326–1234, 800/233–1234 in the U.S.,* ☎ *11/4326–3736.
116 rooms, 50 suites. Restaurant, bar, coffee shop, room
service, pool, health club, concierge, business services,
meeting rooms. AE, DC, MC, V.*

$$$-$$$$ ⊞ **Plaza Francia.** The best-situated small hotel in town, the Plaza Francia overlooks the park of the same name. Rooms are large and have a French feel, with overstuffed pillows, head rolls, and crisp white curtains. Ask for one with a park view, though if traffic noise bothers you, get an inside room. ⊠ *Pasaje E. Schiaffino 2189, 1129,* ☎ ℻ *11/4804–9631. 36 rooms, 14 suites. Room service. AE, DC, MC, V.*

San Telmo

$$ ⊞ **Constitución Palace Hotel.** This hotel is near La Boca and San Telmo in the neighborhood of Constitución (you need to use caution in this area at night). Rooms are stark but you can't beat the price; breakfast is included in the rates. If you're planning any trips out of town, this hotel is right next to one of the city's main train stations, Constitución. ⊠ *Lima 1697, 1138,* ☎ *11/4305–9010,* ℻ *11/4305–9015. 150 rooms. Bar, room service, in-room modem lines, laundry, meeting rooms. AE, DC, MC, V. Subte: Estación Constitución.*

Vicente Lopez

$-$$ ⊞ **Hotel Vicente Lopez.** In the charming and fashionable suburb of Vicente Lopez, this quiet hotel is close to the river and steps from the commuter train, which can bring you to downtown in 15 minutes. Embassies in the suburbs often house visiting guests here. Rooms are clean if minimal. ⊠ *Libertador 902, 1001,* ☎ *11/4797–3773. 30 rooms. Parking, breakfast room. AE, DC, MC, V. Subte: Estación Vicente Lopez.*

5 Nightlife and the Arts

LISTINGS OF EVENTS can be found daily in the English-language *Buenos Aires Herald*, especially in the comprehensive Friday edition. If you read Spanish, check out the more complete weekend section in the Friday edition of *La Nación*.

NIGHTLIFE

It's good to begin with a basic understanding of the Argentine idea of nightlife: A date at 7 PM is considered an afternoon coffee break; theater performances start at 9 PM or 9:30 PM; the last movie begins after midnight; and nightclubs don't begin filling up until 2 AM. Tango, too, gets going after midnight and never seems to stop. Porteños never go early to discos—they wouldn't want to be seen before 2 AM. In fact, even if you wanted to go early, you might not be allowed in: "early evening" hours are often reserved for teenagers, and no one over 18 may be permitted to enter until after midnight. For the most part, Buenos Aires's dance clubs attract young crowds (in the 18–30 age range). The best places to go out are in La Recoleta, Palermo, and Costanera Norte. Note that the subte closes at 10 PM, so if you go out late, either count on taking a taxi home or waiting until 5 AM for the subte to start running again.

Bars and Clubs

BELGRANO

New York City (⊠ Av. Alvarez Thomas 1391, ☎ 11/4555–5559), decorated to look like a spot in downtown Manhattan, is primarily filled with people in their teens and early twenties. **Tobaggo Cigar and Arts Café** (⊠ Alvarez Thomas 138, ☎ 11/4553–5530) is all about cigar culture (and hosts events).

EL CENTRO

Ave Porco (⊠ Av. Corrientes 1980, ☎ 11/4953–7129), in the theater district, has a little bit of everything—a techno dance room, an upstairs lounge, and a back patio. **La Cigale** (⊠ 25 de Mayo 722, ☎ 11/4813–8275) has a large bar to lean up to and good music. For a little Irish-bar atmosphere and some Guinness, check out **Druid In** (⊠ Reconquista 1040, ☎ 11/4312–3688). **Dunn** (⊠ San Martín 986) is a small bar where electronic music is the soundtrack of choice. At **Morocco** (⊠ Hipólito Yrigoyen 851, ☎ 11/4342–6046) you never know when you'll see an impromptu drag show. An older, more refined crowd goes for drinks and cigars to the Marriott's elegant **Plaza Bar** (⊠ Florida 1005, ☎ 11/4318–3000). For a quick tango lesson and a beer, head to **Sedon** (⊠ 25 de Mayo and Córdoba, ☎ 11/4361–0141). **Shamrock** (⊠ Rodríguez Peña 1220, ☎ 11/4812–3584) is an Irish-style bar where an English-speaking expat crowd is often found; happy hour is from 6 to 9.

COSTANERA

Open Plaza Junior (⊠ Av. F. Alcorta, ☎ 11/4782–7204), which caters to a very fashionable crowd, has a sprawling bar, pool tables, a disco, a restaurant, and a shark tank. **Tequila** (⊠ Costanera Norte and La Pampa, ☎ 11/4788–0438) is one of the most happening bars in the city; expect a line out the door.

PALERMO

Buenos Aires News (⊠ Infanta Isabel, ☎ 11/4778–1500) is one of the city's trendiest nightspots—you might even see a model or a rock star. **El Living** (⊠ Marcelo T. de Alvear 1540, ☎ 11/4811–4730) is a trendy disco and bar with lounge chairs and great drinks. **Gallery** (⊠ Azcuénaga 1771, ☎ 11/4807–1652) draws a young crowd with live salsa bands and frozen margaritas; the restaurant, which opens at 8:30, serves rather bland Tex-Mex dishes. The city's most popular disco is **La Morocha** (⊠ Av. Dorrego 3307, ☎ 11/4778–0050); January–March this location is closed, and a branch of it opens at the beach in Uruguay. **Mundo Bizarro** (⊠ Guatemala 4802, ☎ 11/4773–1967) is a cool bar with a hip crowd. **Nero** (⊠ Marcelo T. de Alvear 538, ☎ 11/4313–3458) has a minimalist appeal.

PUERTO MADERO

El Divino (⊠ Cecilia Grierson 225, ☎ 11/4315–2791), in a space that was built to resemble the Sydney Opera House, appeals to an affluent, fashionable set.

LA RECOLETA

Like so many capitals around the world, Buenos Aires has

its own **Hard Rock Café** (⊠ La Recoleta Design Center, Av. Pueyrredón 2501, ☎ 11/4807–7625), serving typical American drinks and snacks; on weekends an irritatingly high cover is charged. **The Spot** (⊠ Ayacucho 1261, ☎ 11/4811–8955) is a cocktail bar with a daily happy hour.

SAN TELMO

One of Buenos Aires's most traditional bars, **Dorrego** (⊠ Defensa 1098, ☎ 11/4361–0141) was once a general store; it's now the place (best in the afternoon) to down Quilmes beers and peanuts.

Gay and Lesbian Bars and Clubs

Right in El Centro, **Angels** (⊠ Viamonte 2168) has several dance floors and attracts a primarily gay and transvestite clientele. **Bunker** (⊠ Anchorena 1170), an old standard, draws a mixed lot. **Confusión** (⊠ Av. Scalabrini Ortíz 1721), in El Centro, hosts techno dance parties until dawn for a gay, lesbian, and transvestite crowd. **Teleny** (⊠ Juncal 2479) has good drinks and live drag shows.

Jazz Clubs

Buenos Aires has serious jazz musicians and enthusiastic audiences. **Café Tortoni** (⊠ Av. de Mayo 825, ☎ 11/4342–4328) has jazz on weekends. **Gazelle Jazz Club** (⊠ Estados Unidos 465, ☎ 11/4361–4685), in San Telmo, is the place to see local and foreign groups. **The Jazz Club** (⊠ La Plaza Complex, Av. Corrientes 1660) often has jazz concerts in the evening and serves good drinks and snacks. **Notorious** (⊠ Av. Callao 966, ☎ 11/4813–6888) has jazz shows several times per week, and when there isn't live music, you can play music on your table's CD player. **Patio Bullrich** (⊠ Av. del Libertador 750) frequently has evening jazz performances. At **Salo** (⊠ Arroyo 1167) jazz and blues are played in a dark, Parislike setting.

THE ARTS

Except for some international short-run performances, tickets to most events are surprisingly easy to get. Tickets can be purchased at the box office of the venue or at various ticket outlets. **Ticketmaster** (☎ 11/4326–9903) sells tickets for events at the Colón, Luna Park, Teatro Globo, and the

Teatro Municipal San Martín, and accepts MasterCard and Visa for phone purchases. **Ticketron** (☎ 11/4321–9700) has tickets to the same venues as Ticketmaster as well as to local theaters and music halls. **Musimundo,** a record store with several branches throughout the city (there's one in every mall) sells tickets for concerts. Note that, like most other businesses in Argentina, theaters take a summer vacation (January–February). To see theater productions in January and February, you may have to drive to the beach! Men usually wear jackets and ties to theater performances, and women also dress accordingly.

Classical Music and Opera

By any standard, the **Teatro Colón** (✉ ticket office: Tucumán 1111, ☎ 11/4382–4784) is one of the world's finest opera houses. Tiered like a wedding cake, the gilt and red-velvet auditorium has unsurpassed acoustics. Pavarotti has said that the Colón has only one thing wrong with it: the acoustics are so good, every mistake can be heard. An everchanging stream of imported talent bolsters the well-regarded local company. The opera season runs from April to November. The **National Symphony** is also headquartered in the Colón Theater and its performances also run from April to November.

Dance

A mixture of passion, sensuality, nostalgia, and melancholy, the tango is the dance of Argentina and Buenos Aires is its capital. Every child learns it, every couple knows it. You can experience the culture of tango everywhere in Buenos Aires: at a show at the world-famous Casablanca, in a spontaneous outburst on Calle Florida, at a glitzy nightclub, or at a neighborhood spot in San Telmo. Opening days and times of tango halls regularly change, so call to verify before you arrive. If you'd prefer to bask in the history of the dance, retrace the footsteps of Carlos Gardel, the tango's great hero (he died in a plane crash in 1935 at the age of 40), in the Mercado del Abasto neighborhood and then visit his grave at the Chacarita Cemetery.

You'll see advertisements for tango performances everywhere. The best performances are at **Casa Blanca** (✉ Balcarce 668, ☎ 11/4331–4621) in San Telmo. **Michelangelo** (✉ Balcarce 433, ☎ 11/4331–9659) combines folk, tango, and international music in a dinner show at its striking, remodeled old warehouse location. A very traditional show takes place at San Telmo's **Viejo Almacén** (✉ Balcarce and Independencia, ☎ 11/4307–6689). More authentic and considerably less expensive tango shows are staged at 10 PM weeknights at the **Gran Café Tortoni** (✉ Av. de Mayo 829, ☎ 11/4342–4328).

Akarense (✉ Donado 1355 at Av. Los Incas, ☎ 11/4651–2121) draws the best dancers to its beautiful hall. You can dance tango Tuesday, Friday, Saturday, and Sunday nights at **Club Almagro** (✉ Medrano 522, ☎ 11/4774–7454) with porteños of all ages who come to enjoy their national dance. **La Galería del Tango Argentino** (✉ Av. Boedo 722) has competitions and shows; tango *fantasía*, a version that allows dancers to show off their abilities, is very popular here. **Ideal** (✉ Suipacha 384, ☎ 11/4601–8234) is less intimidating; people of all ages come here to practice, while teachers offer informal instruction. **Regine's** (✉ Av. Río Bamba 416) is a small place reminiscent of Fellini's *Satyricon*. The very special **Sin Rumbo** (✉ Tamborini 6157, ☎ 11/4571–9577) attracts old *milonga* (a sambalike dance that predates the tango) dancers. The very large **Social Rivadavia** (✉ Av. Rivadavía 6465, ☎ 11/4632–8064) has two dance floors and music mainly from the '40s. **Viejo Correo** (✉ Av. Diaz Velez 4820, ☎ 11/4958–0364) has a more sophisticated atmosphere than most of the other tango spots.

Another place to become one with tango is through a private lesson at the **Estudio Guillermo Alio** (✉ Magalanes 859, ☎ 11/4303–1276); Mr. Alio's daughter, who works in the studio, speaks fluent English. Another place for a lesson is the **Academia Nacional de Tango** (✉ Av. de Mayo 833, ☎ 11/4345–6967) on Monday, Wednesday, and Friday nights at 7:30; don't worry about bringing a partner—they will pair you up if needed.

The tango is not Buenos Aires's only dance: Porteños also gather in droves on weekends to dance to the pulsating beats of samba and salsa. **Salsón** (⊠ Av. Alvarez Thomas 1166, ☏ 11/4637–6970), which is *the* place for salsa in Buenos Aires, has salsa lessons on Wednesday and Friday nights at 9 PM. If you want to learn Brazilian dance, head to **Sudaca** (⊠ Sarmiento 1752, ☏ 11/4371–0802) for a quick samba lesson. **La Trastienda** (⊠ at Balcarce and Belgrano, ☏ 11/4434–2760) is a large dance hall hosting salsa classes and energetic crowds; it also occasionally doubles as a performance space for tango shows.

The **National Ballet Company** is headquartered at the Teatro Colón (☞ Classical Music and Opera, *above*) but gives open-air performances in Palermo in summer. World-class contemporary dance is performed several times a year at the **Teatro San Martín** (⊠ Av. Corrientes 1530, ☏ 11/4374–8611 or 11/4331–7553).

Film

First-run Hollywood movies, Argentine films, and Italian comedies are shown at the more than 50 theaters in the downtown area alone. Most of these are along two parallel streets, Avenida Corrientes and Calle Lavalle. The *Buenos Aires Herald* has daily listings. The names of the films are generally given in Spanish, but English-language films are shown undubbed, with Spanish subtitles. Seats are assigned at movie theaters: When purchasing tickets, you can choose your seat. Ushers, who expect a one-peso tip, show you to your seats if a movie has already begun or if the theater is particularly crowded. Tickets are usually around $7.50, but the first show of the day is half price, and all cinemas are half price all day Wednesday. The following theaters show Argentine and Hollywood films: **Belgrano Multiplex** (⊠ at Obligado and Mendoza, ☏ 11/4781–8183); **Paseo Alcorta** (⊠ at F. Alcorta and Salguero, ☏ 11/4806–5665); and **Puerto Madero** (⊠ Av. M. de Justo 1960, ☏ 11/4315–3008).

Theater

Buenos Aires has some 40 theaters, ranging from those presenting Argentine dramatic works to those showing foreign plays in translation, musicals, and *revistas* (revues) with comedians and dancers known for the brevity of their costumes. **La Plaza** (✉ Av. Corrientes 1660, ☎ 11/4382–4177) is an open-air shopping center with a small outdoor amphitheater and two theaters, along with shops and small restaurants. Publicly supported theater, mime, puppet shows, and dance are performed on the three stages of the municipal theater complex, **Teatro San Martín** (✉ Av. Corrientes 1530, ☎ 11/4374–8611 or 11/4331–7553).

6 Outdoor Activities and Sports

N A 1998 SURVEY conducted by the *Clarin,* the most widely circulated paper in Argentina, thousands of Argentines were asked, "What brings you joy?" Thirteen percent responded that it was money, 20% said their families, and 50% responded soccer. Watching a game in Buenos Aires's Estadio Boca Juniors, you'll see Argentine passion at its most raucous. Being a part of the crowd at Buenos Aires sports events is always thrilling: try the horse races or the city's internationally renowned polo matches. Or you can get active yourself with paddle tennis, an Argentinean favorite, or a leisurely round of golf.

Participant Sports

Athletic Clubs

Athletic clubs in Buenos Aires are not only gyms with weight-lifting equipment, aerobics classes, and pools, but they're also places to participate in organized sports. **Club de Amigos** (⊠ Av. Alcorta, ☎ 11/4801–1213) has pickup soccer games and tennis lessons as well as a gym and a pool. **Coconor** (⊠ Rafael Obligado and Salguero, ☎ 11/4788–5995) is the closest that Buenos Aires comes to a beach club: For $25 per day you can mix and mingle at this sports club with a pool operated by Club Med. **Punta Carrasco** (⊠ Costanera Norte and Sarmiento, ☎ 11/4807–1010) is a sports complex with a swimming pool, tennis courts, organized sports, and lots of people-watching.

Bicycling and Running

It's unusual to see people running on the streets; jogging and biking are usually confined to such parks as the Parque Tres de Febrero in Palermo (there's usually a stand in the park where you can rent bikes) and the Reserva Ecológica (Ecological Reserve; ☞ Off the Beaten Path *in* Puerto Madero, *above*). For an enclosed, bikers-only atmosphere at a nominal admission charge, head to the **Velodromo** (⊠ Av. Tornquist).

Chess

Pursuing a hobby, especially one with such a universal language as chess, is a good way to meet Argentines. It's played at the **Gran Café Tortoni** (⊠ Av. de Mayo 829, ☎ 11/4342–4328); upstairs at the **Confitería Ideal** (⊠ Suipacha 384, ☎ 11/4326–0521); in the mansion wing of the **Park Hyatt Buenos Aires** (☞ Chapter 4); and in the basement lounge of the **Richmond** (⊠ Florida 468, ☎ 11/4322–1341).

Golf

Cancha Municipal de Golf (⊠ Tornquist and Olleros, ☎ 11/4772–7261 or 11/4772–7576) is a public golf course that's 10 minutes from downtown in Palermo. **Costa Salguero** (⊠ Rafael Obligado and Salguero, ☎ 11/4804–2444) is a complete sports and health complex, with a focus on golf. For more information call the **Asociación Argentina de Golf** (Argentine Golf Association, ⊠ Av. Corrientes 538, 11th and 12th floors, ☎ 11/4394–2743). The plush **Miraflores Country Club** (⊠ Ruta Panamericana, Km 35½, ☎ 3327/454–800), in the suburb of Garín (follow signs on the highway to the town of Pilar), is open to nonmembers on Tuesday, Saturday, and Sunday, for a $30 greens fee.

Paddle Tennis

Paddle tennis, a typical Argentine game that is sort of a cross between tennis and squash, is popular with all ages. The city has hundreds of courts. **Circuito KDT** (⊠ Salguero 3450, ☎ 11/4802–2619) has excellent courts available by reservation. **Recoleta Squash** (⊠ Ayacucho 1669, ☎ 11/4801–3848) is open to nonmembers, but you must reserve in advance.

Spa

Buenos Aires's **Colmegña Spa** (⊠ Sarmiento 839, ☎ 11/4326–1257) is as relaxing as it gets. For $99 you can have a full day at the spa, including a Turkish bath, body peel, massage, hair, and lunch. An appointment is essential; it's open Tuesday–Saturday 11–8.

Squash

A good place to play is at the central **Olimpia Cancilería** (⊠ Esmeralda 1042, ☎ 11/4313–7375), which also has racquetball courts. Another possibility is **Recoleta Squash** (⊠ Ayacucho 1669, ☎ 11/4801–3848).

Tennis

Many of the athletic clubs (☞ *above*) have tennis courts that you can use for a fee. There are public tennis courts at the **Buenos Aires Lawn Tennis Club** (⊠ Av. Olleros 1510, ☎ 11/4772–9227). Arrangements can be made through the executive offices at the **Sheraton** (⊠ San Martín 1225, ☎ 11/4318–9309) to play on the hotel's courts for $15 per hour.

Spectator Sports

Boxing and Wrestling

Boxing and wrestling matches are held in **Luna Park** (⊠ Bouchard 465, ☎ 11/4311–1990 or 11/4312–2538), an indoor arena. Check the *Buenos Aires Herald* for details.

Cricket

Cricket is played at the suburban **Hurlingham Club** (⊠ Av. J. A. Roca 1411, ☎ 11/4665–0401) and other Anglo-Argentine enclaves. Check the *Herald* for information.

Horse Racing

Historians consider the strong Thoroughbreds from Argentina one of the factors that favored the British in the South African Boer War. Argentines on spending binges brought, and occasionally still bring, the best stock in the world home to breed, and swift Argentine horses are prized throughout the world. Although the past 40 years of rough economic times have handicapped the Thoroughbred industry, Argentine horses still win their share of races in North America and Europe. There are two main tracks in Buenos Aires; check the *Buenos Aires Herald* for schedules. Generally, races take place on Wednesday and Saturday at **Hipódromo de San Isidro** (⊠ Av. Márquez 504, ☎ 11/4743–4010), in the historic suburb of San Isidro. Closer to downtown, in Palermo, is the dirt track at the traditional **Hipódromo Argentino** (⊠ Av. del Libertador 4000, ☎ 11/4777–9009).

Polo

Polo, like soccer, was introduced by the British. Natural riding skills and an abundance of good horses quickly produced the world's top players, who, like soccer players, are paid enormous sums to compete for foreign teams. Argentine polo ponies, known for their quickness, intelligence, and strength, are sold the world over, as are race, show-jumping, and dressage horses. The best polo matches are in November, as are other equestrian events such as horse racing, show jumping, and dressage, all of which attract dedicated devotees both local and international.

Argentine polo has been compared to a performance of the Bolshoi Ballet in its heyday—a strenuous display of stunning athletic showmanship. At the **Canchas Nacionales** (National Fields), on Avenida Dorrego in the barrio of Palermo in Buenos Aires, sold-out crowds cheer on national heroes. There are two seasons: March–May and September–December. Tickets can be purchased in advance through ticket agencies or on the day of the event; general admission is about $7. The best teams compete in the Argentine Open Championships in November. For match information contact the **Asociación Argentina de Polo** (⊠ H. Yrigoyen 636, 1st floor, Apt. A, ☎ 11/4331–4646).

Soccer

River Plate, Boca Juniors, and Maradona—these names are as familiar to Argentines as the Dodgers, Yankees, and Babe Ruth are to Americans. They are the subject of fiery dispute, suicidal despair, love, hate, pride, and all the emotions that soccer arouses in this nation whose blue-and-white striped jerseys have flashed across TV screens since it won the 1978 and 1986 World Championships.

Soccer is a huge part of Porteño life. Soccer matches are held year-round; to see Argentine passion, go to a game. Sitting among tens of thousands of roaring fans can be a disconcerting experience, especially if you get swept off your perch in the bleachers as a human wave slides five rows back and forth to cheer a goal. For this reason, it's recommended that you pay for a seat (around $40–$60) rather than opting for the often chaotic and frequently dangerous (but cheaper) standing-room section. Passions run especially high when La Boca's Boca Juniors take on their arch-rivals, River Plate, from the upper-crust district of Belgrano. (The rivalry has a deeper political and socioeconomic significance: Supporters of Boca are drawn from Buenos Aires's working class, while River Plate is traditionally the team of the city's more urbane middle and upper classes.) Major games are played at the **Estadio Boca Juniors** (⊠ Brandsen 805). Tickets can be purchased at the stadium before the game.

In case you want to see the world.

At American Express, we're here to make your journey a smooth one. So we have over 1,700 travel service locations in over 130 countries ready to help. What else would you expect from the world's largest travel agency?

do more Travel

Call 1 800 AXP-3429 or visit
www.americanexpress.com/travel

In case you want to be welcomed there.

We're here to see that you're always welcomed at establishments everywhere. That's why millions of people carry the American Express® Card – for peace of mind, confidence, and security, around the world or just around the corner.

do more **AMERICAN EXPRESS**®

Cards

In case you're running low.

We're here to help with more than 190,000 Express Cash locations around the world. In order to enroll, just call American Express at 1 800 CASH-NOW before you start your vacation.

do more

Express Cash

And in case you'd rather be safe than sorry.

We're here with American Express® Travelers Cheques. They're the safe way to carry money on your vacation, because if they're ever lost or stolen you can get a refund, practically anywhere or anytime. To find the nearest place to buy Travelers Cheques, call 1 800 495-1153. Another way we help you do more.

do more® **AMERICAN EXPRESS**

Travelers Cheques

Tennis

Guillermo Vilas, José Luis Clerc, and Gabriela Sabatini are all products of local clubs. Most professional tennis matches are played at the **Buenos Aires Lawn Tennis Club** (⊠ Av. Olleros 1510, ☎ 11/4772–9227).

7 Shopping

THERE WAS A TIME not so long ago when Argentine families went to Miami to purchase quality goods. But the situation has changed with the lifting of trade bans, and items are becoming much more widely available. Clothing made in Argentina is generally not that well constructed, though this is improving, too.

When shopping in Buenos Aires as a foreigner, keep your receipts; the 21% VAT tax, added to almost every purchase you'll make, is entirely refundable for purchases of more than $200. When you depart, plan enough time to visit the return desk at the airport to obtain your refund.

Areas

Avenida Santa Fe
Downtown Avenida Santa Fe is great for browsing: lining it are hundreds of little boutiques and bustling cafés. It's a good place to find fashionable, reasonably priced clothes.

Calle Florida
Crowded, pedestrians-only Calle Florida, the main downtown shopping street, is lined with McDonald's (there are four and counting along this 10-block street), persistent vendors, and stores of all kinds. It's a good place to go first to establish a quality and price standard, as well as for last-minute souvenirs and food especially packaged for plane trips. The street is also home to the city's best bookstores. Keep in mind that the closer you get to Plaza San Martín, the better the offerings.

La Recoleta
With its designer boutiques and expensive stores, concentrated on Avenida Alvear, and Calle Quintana, La Recoleta is the finest area to shop in the city.

San Telmo
San Telmo is the antiques shopping district. Many old homes have been converted into shops, like those in the Pasaje de la Defensa (Defense Alley). One of these is an elaborate Italianate house built in the 1850s that once belonged to the Ezeiza family (namesake of the town where your plane

will land, if you fly into Argentina). At the turn of the 20th century it was transformed into a tenement for immigrants and now houses several dozen antiques vendors.

Malls

Abasto (✉ Av. Corrientes 3200) is a shopping mall, with the usual clothing stores and restaurants, in a renovated old marketplace, which is modernized inside but has the original facade.

Alto Palermo (✉ corner of Av. Santa Fe and Av. Colonel Diaz, subte: Line D to Estación Bulnes) has three floors of clothes shops, cafés, and toy and book stores right on the bustling Avenida Santa Fe.

Galerías Pacífico (Pacífico Shopping Center; ✉ Florida 753, at Av. Córdoba) is in the former headquarters of the Buenos Aires–Pacific Railway, a building designed during Buenos Aires's turn-of-the-20th-century golden age in the style of Milan's Gallerie Vittorio Emanuele. In 1992 it was transformed into a glossy, multilevel California-style shopping center (in an earlier renovation a large skylight dome was added, and five leading Argentine artists were commissioned to paint murals). Currently managed by a consortium owned by George Soros, the Galerías Pacífico stands out as one of the finer places to shop as well as to have a quick lunch on busy Calle Florida.

Paseo Alcorta (✉ Av. Alcorta and Salguero), in Palermo, has chic Argentine clothing stores for men and women, as well as such internationally known stores as Christian Dior and Yves St. Laurent, a four-screen movie theater, and a food court.

Patio Bullrich (✉ Av. del Libertador 740), near the Park Hyatt, has some of the finest and priciest shops in town as well as a six-screen movie theater. This multilevel mall was once the headquarters for the Bullrich family's auction house, Buenos Aires's most renowned auctioneers. The basement held hundreds of head of cattle during auctions, and the upper floors were dedicated to selling paintings, furniture, and antiques, including portraits of the livestock and their owners. If you look carefully at the walls on the upper level, you can still see stucco heads of steers emerging in relief. The auction house now functions next door

under the name of Posadas (☞ Art and Antiques, *below*).
Solar de la Abadía (⊠ Marie Luis Campos and Arcos) is
a great place to pick up souvenirs, buy trendy clothes, or
have a snack. As it's on the border of Belgrano and the Cañitas section of Palermo, it's also a good place to begin or
end a walk around the area. It's about a 10-minute walk
from the Museo Nacional del Hombre, and about 20 minutes from Plaza Belgrano.

Markets

Open-air markets can be one of the best shopping experi-
ences in Buenos Aires (and can be good places to find souvenirs). The markets listed below are open all day on
weekends, though none really gets going until the early afternoon. Feel free to try to bargain: often it works, and if
it doesn't, you can be assured of finding a similar item at
another stall. The markets all carry basically the same types
of goods, but if there's one not to miss, it's the San Telmo
Market: ongoing entertainment, such as tango dancing, keeps
the atmosphere particularly energetic.
Belgrano Square (⊠ Juramento and Vuelta de Obligado,
subte: Line D to end). **Recoleta Feria** (⊠ Av. Libertador and
Av. Pueyrredón). **San Telmo** (⊠ Plaza Dorrego). **Vuelta de
Rocha handicraft market** (⊠ Av. Pedro de Mendoza and
Caminito Palos).

Specialty Shops

Art and Antiques

Most antiques shops are grouped together in San Telmo (☞
Areas, *above*). The city's largest auction house, **Posadas** (⊠
Posadas 1227, ☎ 11/4327–025 or 11/4815–3573) has fur-
nishings and artwork from many local estates.

Bookstores

Numerous bookstores can be found along Calle Florida.
El Atheneo (⊠ Florida 340, ☎ 11/4340–4325) is perhaps
the most famous, and sells a wide selection of works by Argentine authors, and classics and best-sellers in English, as
well as beautiful souvenir coffee-table books depicting the
tango and other scenes from Argentina.

Clothing

European designer shops are mostly concentrated along
Avenida Alvear and Calle Quintana. Chain stores selling
trendy (and often very skimpy) clothing are found all over
Buenos Aires. Most of these stores are in malls (☞ Malls,
above) as well as along Avenida Santa Fe 800–1500 in the
Plaza San Martín area and along Avenida Cabildo 1600–
2200 in Belgrano. **Chocolate** has good quality women's
clothes that appeal to a twenty-something crowd. **Ona
Saez** sells both men's and women's casual and trendy nightclub clothing. **Paula Cahan D'Anvers** sells more conservative, though very small, women's clothing for casual
occasions and work. **Via Vai** is a great place for separates,
like that sundress or sweater you may have forgotten to pack.
Vitamina is aimed at younger shoppers.

Handicrafts

Mercado de las Luces (⊠ Peru and Alsina, subte: Line E to
Estación Bolívar) is a small store selling all kinds of hand-
made souvenirs; note that many are overpriced (the same
items can sometimes be purchased for less in the outdoor
markets in Belgrano and San Telmo). **Patio del Cabildo** (⊠
Av. de Mayo and Bolívar), a crafts store in the Cabildo Museum, sells traditional souvenirs and artwork; it's only
open Thursday and Friday 11–8.

Jewelry

The gold district in Buenos Aires is concentrated in and
around **Calle Libertad,** between Avenidas Corrientes and Rivadavía: Here you can find inexpensive gold jewelry (mostly
18K). Bargaining is expected and you should watch out for
fake stones. An honest jeweler will usually divulge the pre-
ciousness of a stone if asked, but if you don't ask, they won't
tell. Emeralds from Brazil can be a bargain. One semiprecious
stone, *rodocrosita,* known as the "rose of the Inca," is na-
tive only to Argentina; these range from pink to ruby red.
Antonio Belgiorno (⊠ Av. Santa Fe 1347, ☎ 11/4811–
1117) is a top silversmith who creates beautiful, quality silver pieces. Decorated sculptures of birds in flight from
Cousino (⊠ Paraguay 631, 3rd floor, Suite A, ☎ 11/4312–
2336; ⊠ Sheraton Hotel, ☞ Chapter 4) are exhibited in
the National Museum of Decorative Arts. **Guthman** (⊠ Viamonte 597, ☎ 11/4312–2471) has an acclaimed selection

of jewelry. Internationally renowned **H. Stern** (⊠ in Sheraton, Plaza, Hyatt, Inter-Continental, and Alvear Palace hotels; ☞ Chapter 4) is a good place for fine Argentine jewelry.

Leather

Argentina's reputation for fine leather goods is occasionally well deserved. The leather is very high quality, but sometimes craftsmanship is lacking. You can find items made of cowhide, kidskin, pigskin, sheepskin, lizard, snake, and porcupine in an array of colors. Clothing styles range from conservative to hip—everything from bikinis to evening gowns. Prices for leather goods are generally better than abroad, but be sure to check the quality and stitching before you buy. **Casa López** (⊠ M. T. de Alvear 640, ☎ 11/4311–3044) carries jackets and bags. Polo equipment and saddles can be found at **H. Merlo** (⊠ Juncal 743). **La Martina** (⊠ Paraguay 661, ☎ 11/4311–5963) carries furnishings for the discriminating equestrian. **Murillo 666** (⊠ Murillo 666, ☎ 11/4855–2024 has a wide selection of women's bags and jackets at good prices. For briefcases and other leather bags, try **Pullman** (⊠ in the Galerías Pacífico, ☎ 11/4325–4111). **Rossi y Caruso** (⊠ Av. Santa Fe 1601, ☎ 11/4811–1538) has the best in riding equipment as well as handbags, clothing, shoes, and boots; King Juan Carlos of Spain and many other celebrities are customers here.

Sheepskin and Wool

Argentina has traditionally been the world's largest exporter of wool. Several big-name Italian designers such as Benetton get their wool from here. **IKS** (⊠ Alisa Moro de Justo 2040, 1st floor, ☎ 11/4311–4747) is a factory outlet for sweaters. **Silvia y Mario** (⊠ M. T. de Alvear 550), another downtown outlet, stocks a huge selection of cashmere and very elegant two-piece knit dresses. Sheepskin jackets at **Ciudad de Cuero** (⊠ Florida 940) would make the Marlboro man leap off his mount to purchase a winter's supply.

Shoes

For men's loafers, **Guido** (⊠ Florida 704) is Argentina's favorite. For men's and women's shoes that look great and last forever, try **López Taibo** (⊠ Av. Corrientes 350, ☎ 11/4328–2132). Shoes and boots can be found at **Rossi y Caruso** (⊠ Av. Santa Fe 1601, ☎ 11/4811–1538).

SPANISH VOCABULARY

Words and Phrases

	English	Spanish	Pronun-ciation
Basics			
	Yes/no	Sí/no	see/no
	Please	Por favor	pore fah-**vore**
	May I?	¿Me permite?	may pair-**mee**-tay
	Thank you (very much)	(Muchas) gracias	(**moo**-chas) **grah**-see-as
	You're welcome	De nada	day **nah**-dah
	Excuse me	Con permiso	con pair-**mee**-so
	Pardon me	¿Perdón?	pair-**dohn**
	Could you tell me?	¿Podría decirme?	po-dree-ah deh-**seer**-meh
	I'm sorry	Lo siento	lo see-**en**-to
	Good morning!	¡Buenos días!	**bway**-nohs **dee**-ahs
	Good afternoon!	¡Buenas tardes!	**bway**-nahs **tar**-dess
	Good evening!	¡Buenas noches!	**bway**-nahs **no**-chess
	Goodbye!	¡Adiós!/¡Hasta luego!	ah-dee-**ohss**/**ah**-stah-**lwe**-go
	Mr./Mrs.	Señor/Señora	sen-**yor**/sen-**yohr**-ah
	Miss	Señorita	sen-yo-**ree**-tah
	Pleased to meet you	Mucho gusto	**moo**-cho **goose**-to
	How are you?	¿Cómo está usted?	**ko**-mo es-**tah** oo-**sted**
	Very well, thank you.	Muy bien, gracias.	**moo**-ee bee-**en**, **grah**-see-as

	And you?	¿Y usted?	ee oos-**ted**
	Hello (on the telephone)	Diga	**dee**-gah

Numbers

1	un, uno	oon, **oo**-no
2	dos	dos
3	tres	tress
4	cuatro	**kwah**-tro
5	cinco	**sink**-oh
6	seis	saice
7	siete	see-**et**-eh
8	ocho	**o**-cho
9	nueve	new-**eh**-vey
10	diez	dee-**es**
11	once	**ohn**-seh
12	doce	**doh**-seh
13	trece	**treh**-seh
14	catorce	ka-**tohr**-seh
15	quince	**keen**-seh
16	dieciséis	dee-**es**-ee-**saice**
17	diecisiete	dee-**es**-ee-see-**et**-eh
18	dieciocho	dee-**es**-ee-**o**-cho
19	diecinueve	**dee-es**-ee-new-**ev**-ah
20	veinte	**vain**-teh
21	veinte y uno/veintiuno	**vain**-te-**oo**-noh
30	treinta	**train**-tah
32	treinta y dos	train-tay-**dohs**
40	cuarenta	kwah-**ren**-tah
43	cuarenta y tres	kwah-**ren**-tay-**tress**
50	cincuenta	seen-**kwen**-tah
54	cincuenta y cuatro	seen-**kwen**-tay **kwah**-tro
60	sesenta	sess-**en**-tah

65	sesenta y cinco	sess-**en**-tay **seen**-ko
70	setenta	set-**en**-tah
76	setenta y seis	set-**en**-tay **saice**
80	ochenta	oh-**chen**-tah
87	ochenta y siete	oh-**chen**-tay see-**yet**-eh
90	noventa	no-**ven**-tah
98	noventa y ocho	no-**ven**-tah-**o**-choh
100	cien	see-**en**
101	ciento uno	see-**en**-toh **oo**-noh
200	doscientos	doh-see-**en**-tohss
500	quinientos	keen-**yen**-tohss
700	setecientos	set-eh-see-**en**-tohss
900	novecientos	no-veh-see-**en**-tohss
1,000	mil	meel
2,000	dos mil	dohs meel
1,000,000	un millón	oon meel-**yohn**

Colors

black	negro	**neh**-groh
blue	azul	ah-**sool**
brown	café	kah-**feh**
green	verde	**ver**-deh
pink	rosa	**ro**-sah
purple	morado	mo-**rah**-doh
orange	naranja	na-**rahn**-hah
red	rojo	**roh**-hoh
white	blanco	**blahn**-koh
yellow	amarillo	ah-mah-**ree**-yoh

Days of the Week

| Sunday | domingo | doe-**meen**-goh |

Monday	lunes	**loo**-ness
Tuesday	martes	**mahr**-tess
Wednesday	miércoles	me-**air**-koh-less
Thursday	jueves	hoo-**ev**-ess
Friday	viernes	vee-**air**-ness
Saturday	sábado	**sah**-bah-doh

Months

January	enero	eh-**neh**-roh
February	febrero	feh-**breh**-roh
March	marzo	**mahr**-soh
April	abril	ah-**breel**
May	mayo	**my**-oh
June	junio	**hoo**-nee-oh
July	julio	**hoo**-lee-yoh
August	agosto	ah-**ghost**-toh
September	septiembre	sep-tee-**em**-breh
October	octubre	oak-**too**-breh
November	noviembre	no-vee-**em**-breh
December	diciembre	dee-see-**em**-breh

Useful Phrases

Do you speak English?	¿Habla usted inglés?	**ah**-blah oos-**ted** in-**glehs**
I don't speak Spanish	No hablo español	no **ah**-bloh es-pahn-**yol**
I don't understand (you)	No entiendo	no en-tee-**en**-doh
I understand (you)	Entiendo	en-tee-**en**-doh
I don't know	No sé	no seh
I am American/British	Soy americano (americana)/inglés(a)	soy ah-meh-ree-**kah**-no (ah-meh-ree-**kah**-nah)/in-**glehs**(ah)

What's your name?	¿Cómo se llama usted?	koh-mo seh **yah**-mah oos-**ted**
My name is . . .	Me llamo . . .	may **yah**-moh
What time is it?	¿Qué hora es?	keh **o**-rah es
It is one, two, three . . . o'clock.	Es la una. . . . Son las dos, tres	es la **oo**-nah/sohn lahs dohs, tress
Yes, please/No, thank you	Sí, por favor/No, gracias	**see** pohr fah-**vor**/no **grah**-see-us
How?	¿Cómo?	**koh**-mo
When?	¿Cuándo?	**kwahn**-doh
This/Next week	Esta semana/ la semana que entra	**es**-teh seh-**mah**-nah/lah seh-**mah**-nah keh **en**-trah
This/Next month	Este mes/el próximo mes	**es**-teh mehs/el **proke**-see-mo mehs
This/Next year	Este año/el año que viene	**es**-teh **ahn**-yo/el **ahn**-yo keh vee-**yen**-ay
Yesterday/today/ tomorrow	Ayer/hoy/mañana	ah-**yehr**/oy/ mahn-**yah**-nah
This morning/ afternoon	Esta mañana/ tarde	**es**-tah mahn-**yah**-nah/ **tar**-deh
Tonight	Esta noche	**es**-tah **no**-cheh
What?	¿Qué?	keh
What is it?	¿Qué es esto?	keh es **es**-toh
Why?	¿Por qué?	pore **keh**
Who?	¿Quién?	kee-**yen**
Where is . . . ?	¿Dónde está . . . ?	**dohn**-deh es-**tah**

the train station?	la estación del tren?	la es-tah-see-**on** del **train**
the subway station?	la estación del Tren subterráneo?	la es-ta-see-**on** del trehn soob-tair-**ron**-a-o
the bus stop?	la parada del autobus?	la pah-**rah**-dah del oh-toh-**boos**
the post office?	la oficina de correos?	la oh-fee-**see**-nah deh koh-**reh**-os
the bank?	el banco?	el **bahn**-koh
the hotel?	el hotel?	el oh-**tel**
the store?	la tienda?	la tee-**en**-dah
the cashier?	la caja?	la **kah**-hah
the museum?	el museo?	el moo-**seh**-oh
the hospital?	el hospital?	el ohss-pee-**tal**
the elevator?	el ascensor?	el ah-**sen**-sohr
the bathroom?	el baño?	el **bahn**-yoh
Here/there	Aquí/allá	ah-**key**/ah-**yah**
Open/closed	Abierto/cerrado	ah-bee-**er**-toh/ser-**ah**-doh
Left/right	Izquierda/derecha	iss-key-**er**-dah/dare-**eh**-chah
Straight ahead	Derecho	dare-**eh**-choh
Is it near/far?	¿Está cerca/lejos?	es-**tah sehr**-kah/**leh**-hoss
I'd like . . . a room	Quisiera . . . un cuarto/una habitación	kee-see-ehr-ah oon **kwahr**-toh/**oo**-nah ah-bee-tah-see-**on**
the key	la llave	lah **yah**-veh
a newspaper	un periódico	oon pehr-ee-**oh**-dee-koh

a stamp	un sello de correo	oon **seh**-yo dehkoh-**reh**-oh
I'd like to buy . . .	Quisiera comprar . . .	kee-see-**ehr**-ah kohm-**prahr**
cigarettes	cigarrillos	ce-ga-**ree**-yohs
matches	cerillos	ser-**ee**-ohs
a dictionary	un diccionario	oon deek-see-oh-**nah**-ree-oh
soap	jabón	hah-**bohn**
sunglasses	gafas de sol	**ga**-fahs deh sohl
suntan lotion	loción bronceadora	loh-see-**ohn** brohn-seh-ah-**do**-rah
a map	un mapa	oon **mah**-pah
a magazine	una revista	**oon**-ah reh-**veess**-tah
paper	papel	pah-**pel**
envelopes	sobres	**so**-brehs
a postcard	una tarjeta postal	**oon**-ah tar-**het**-ah post-**ahl**
How much is it?	¿Cuánto cuesta?	**kwahn**-toh **kwes**-tah
It's expensive/ cheap	Está caro/barato	es-**tah kah**-roh/bah-**rah**-toh
A little/a lot	Un poquito/ mucho	oon poh-**kee**-toh/**moo**-choh
More/less	Más/menos	mahss/**men**-ohss
Enough/too much/too little	Suficiente/ demasiado/ muy poco	soo-fee-see-**en**-teh/deh-mah-see-**ah**-doh/**moo**-ee**poh**-koh
Telephone	Teléfono	tel-**ef**-oh-no
Telegram	Telegrama	teh-leh-**grah**-mah

I am ill	Estoy enfermo(a)	es-**toy** en-**fehr**-moh (mah)
Please call a doctor	Por favor llame a un medico	pohr fah-**vor** **ya**-meh ah oon **med**-ee-koh
Help!	¡Auxilio! ¡Ayuda! ¡Socorro!	owk-**see**-lee-oh/ah-**yoo**-dah/soh-**kohr**-roh
Fire!	¡Incendio!	en-**sen**-dee-oo
Caution!/Look out!	¡Cuidado!	kwee-**dah**-doh

On the Road

Avenue	Avenida	ah-ven-**ee**-dah
Broad, tree-lined boulevard	Bulevar	boo-leh-**var**
Fertile plain	Vega	**veh**-gah
Highway	Carretera	car-reh-**ter**-ah
Mountain pass, Street	Puerto Calle	poo-**ehr**-toh **cah**-yeh
Waterfront promenade	Rambla	**rahm**-blah
Wharf	Embarcadero	em-bar-cah-**deh**-ro

In Town

Cathedral	Catedral	cah-teh-**dral**
Church	Templo/Iglesia	**tem**-plo/ee-**glehs**-see-ah
City hall	Casa de gobierno	kah-sah deh go-bee-**ehr**-no
Door, gate	Puerta portón	poo-**ehr**-tah por-**ton**
Entrance/exit	Entrada/salida	en-**trah**-dah/sah-**lee**-dah

Inn, rustic bar, or restaurant	Taverna	tah-**vehr**-nah
Main square	Plaza principal	plah-thah prin-see-**pahl**
Market	Mercado	mer-**kah**-doh
Neighborhood	Barrio	**bahr**-ree-o
Traffic circle	Glorieta	glor-ee-**eh**-tah
Wine cellar, wine bar, or wine shop	Bodega	boh-**deh**-gah

Dining Out

A bottle of . . .	Una botella de . . .	**oo**-nah bo-**teh**-yah deh
A cup of . . .	Una taza de . . .	**oo**-nah **tah**-thah deh
A glass of . . .	Un vaso de . . .	oon **vah**-so deh
Ashtray	Un cenicero	oon sen-ee-**seh**-roh
Bill/check	La cuenta	lah **kwen**-tah
Bread	El pan	el pahn
Breakfast	El desayuno	el deh-sah-**yoon**-oh
Butter	La mantequilla	lah man-teh-**key**-yah
Cheers!	¡Salud!	sah-**lood**
Cocktail	Un aperitivo	oon ah-pehr-ee-**tee**-voh
Dinner	La cena	lah **seh**-nah
Dish	Un plato	oon **plah**-toh
Menu of the day	Menú del día	meh-**noo** del **dee**-ah
Enjoy!	¡Buen provecho!	bwehn pro-**veh**-cho
Fixed-price menu	Menú fijo o turistico	meh-**noo** fee-hoh oh too-**ree**-stee-coh
Fork	El tenedor	el ten-eh-**dor**

Is the tip included?	¿Está incluida la propina?	es-**tah** in-cloo-**ee**-dah lah pro-**pee**-nah
Knife	El cuchillo	el koo-**chee**-yo
Large portion of savory snacks	Raciónes	rah-see-**oh**-nehs
Lunch	La comida	lah koh-**mee**-dah
Menu	La carta, el menú	lah **cart**-ah, el meh-**noo**
Napkin	La servilleta	lah sehr-vee-**yet**-ah
Pepper	La pimienta	lah pee-me-**en**-tah
Please give me . . .	Por favor déme . . .	pore fah-**vor** **deh**-meh
Salt	La sal	lah sahl
Savory snacks	Tapas	**tah**-pahs
Spoon	Una cuchara	**oo**-nah koo-**chah**-rah
Sugar	El azúcar	el ah-**thu**-kar
Waiter!/Waitress!	¡Por favor Señor/Señorita!	pohr fah-**vor** sen-**yor**/sen-yor-**ee**-tah

INDEX

NOTES

NOTES

NOTES

NOTES

NOTES

NOTES

NOTES